C0-AZT-805

Fifty Hikes in Massachusetts

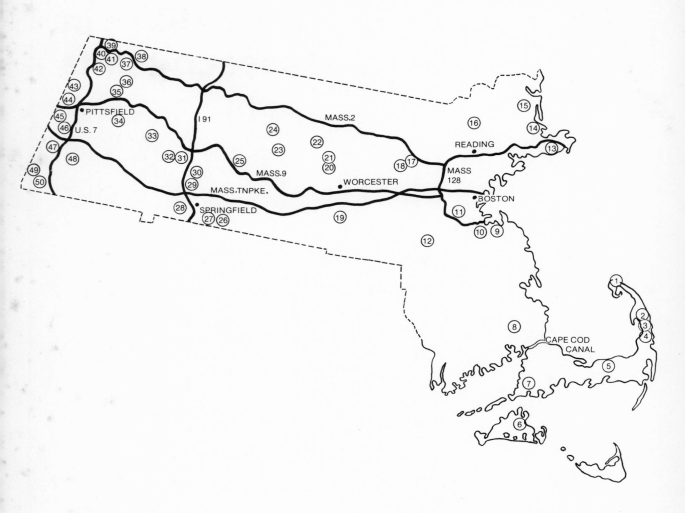

Paul and Ruth Sadlier

Fifty Hikes in Massachusetts

Coastal Walks, Inland Treks, and Mountain Hikes
From Cape Cod to the Berkshires

With Photographs and Maps by the Authors

New Hampshire Publishing Company
Somersworth

An Invitation to the Reader

If you find that conditions have changed along these
trails, please let the author and publisher know so
that corrections may be made in future editions.
Address all correspondence:

Editor, *50 Hikes*
New Hampshire Publishing Company
Post Office Box 70
Somersworth, NH 03878

Copyright © 1975 by Paul and Ruth Sadlier

All rights reserved

Published by the New Hampshire Publishing
Company, 9 Orange Street, Somersworth, NH 03878

Library of Congress catalog card number: 74-33817

ISBN 0-912274-47-6

Manufactured in the United States of America

First printing, May 1975
Second printing, June 1976
Third printing, May 1978
Fourth printing, September 1980

Contents

Introduction

Although usually looked upon as an integral part of the Boston-Washington megalopolis, Massachusetts contains a surprisingly large number of hiking trails and natural areas. Picturesque mountains, most snuggled along the state's western border, retain their pristine beauty and provide both challenges and rewards for today's hikers. Wooded uplands offer a peaceful seclusion. Trails along marshlands and the ocean drench the senses with fresh salt breezes and reminders of the Bay State's maritime past. Wildlife sanctuaries and refuges provide habitats for countless animals and the chance to glimpse many of these creatures in natural settings.

The Fifty Hikes

Variety is the key to the excursions in this book. We selected hikes that would appeal to a wide range of people—and to people with a wide range of interests. There are braille trails (specifically

The Authors

designed for the blind but equally fascinating to sighted persons because of their emphasis on the non-visual senses), a holly reservation, botanic trails, state and town forests, bird sanctuaries, wildlife refuges, mountain, upland, and ocean trails, historic sites, and one island trip. All hikes follow established trails that are either well marked or easily recognized.

Hikers with varying degrees of ability and experience can use and enjoy this book. To help you determine appropriate outings, we've included classification criteria at the beginning of each trek. They are:

Class I:
Mostly flat-to-gradual grade, no obstacles.
Class II:
Mostly gradual-to-moderate grade; possible isolated steep sections.
Class III:
Gradual-to-mostly-moderate grade; occasional steep sections possibly requiring minimal use of hands.
Class IV:
Moderate-to-steep grade; care

required along steep sections; use of hands helpful at times.

Because the Massachusetts topography is not particularly rugged, beginners should consider most hikes within their reach. Likewise, more experienced hikers will appreciate the diversified experiences awaiting their discovery along less arduous trails.

You will also find frequent mileage checks using obvious landmarks to tell you how far you've gone—or have to go.

When consulting the map for each hike, note that the top always represents north.

Elevation, Vertical Rise, Distance, Hiking Time

These categories (plus "class" described above) appear at the beginning of each hike and give a capsule projection of what lies ahead. Elevation and vertical rise do not appear at the top of some hikes in Classes I and II, indicating that these guidelines are too insignificant to be included.

The "elevation" is that appearing on U.S. Geological Survey (U.S.G.S.) maps and on signs posted atop summits. However, if you climb a 3,500-foot mountain it does not mean you've risen 3,500 feet upon reaching the top. You must subtract the height of your starting point from the mountain's height to determine the actual rise in elevation. "Vertical rise" provides this information. Sometimes you will climb up and down valleys before ascending to a summit. Those preliminary upward climbs are included in the vertical-rise figure. In short, we are using "vertical rise" to indicate the total amount of *upward* climbing entailed in a hike. As a general rule, you can expect that the greater the vertical rise per mile, the more strenuous the hike.

"Distance" gives the exact mileage from start to finish. All the trips return you to your starting point via a loop or a single "up-and-back" trail.

Remember that "hiking time" means just that; it does not include long rests, lunch, or observation stops. (You could easily double, triple, or even quadruple the listed hiking time while enjoying these fifty hikes.) After a couple of excursions you should know how your pace compares with our steady-but-leisurely one.

Backpacking

"Unless it (the Appalachian Trail) follows the highest and steepest ridges, requiring effort to walk it, and unless in all more or less populous districts it is without shelter cabins, it will become just one more place to go, it will invite hooligans and create litter and ultimately it will defeat the ends of those who have - "projected it."* William Pritchard Eaton uttered these words before the blazing of the Appalachian Trail in Massachusetts. Unheeded at the time, his sage prophecy has come true. Today the Appalachian Trail suffers from overuse and the litter and abuse of uncaring individuals.

We have not included backpacking trips among our fifty hikes because of current over-

*The Springfield *Sunday Union and Republican,* Jan. 21, 1928.

crowded trail conditions and the lack of regularly spaced shelters. The Appalachian Mountain Club in Massachusetts has considered halting the repair and rebuilding of vandalized trail shelters and, possibly, eliminating these structures entirely. This move would help to attract only those people who appreciate the agreeable rigors of roughing it in the out-of-doors. These are the people who don't mind the cost of an extended wilderness visit—i.e. toting bed and board on their backs —and who care enough to leave no sign of their presence.

Rules and Regulations

You do not leave these behind when departing from civilization. Most rules and regulations have been developed to help us preserve natural areas and the wildlife living therein. Philosophies such as "leaving nothing but footprints" carry important messages, but are not specific enough to check the careless rush of mankind.

Many areas, especially those maintained by organized groups such as the Trustees of Reservations (a non-profit group which preserves interesting areas for public use), the Massachusetts Audubon Society, and the National Park Service, contain posted signs and printed literature detailing "dos and don'ts." These suggestions should be followed in all areas described in this book.

Seasonal Hiking

Your ability and preference provide the only limits to the hiking season in Massachusetts. When the leaves start to turn you are treated to one of nature's wonders. Cool air and rainbow colors combine to give you a "natural high." As the air gets crisper and leaves tumble, light snow blankets the trails. Not deep enough to be a hindrance, this covering is dotted with animal tracks which unfold like a story as you walk along. Heavy snows mean it's time to break out the snowshoes. (We don't suggest that novices begin their hiking in winter.)

Spring brings sprouting greens and lingering reminders of winter. Remember that snow may remain at higher elevations into May. Trails may be cluttered by trees and branches, and

rutted in spots. June and July offer plenty of sunny days— and bugs. Take along plenty of insect repellent and, if on Cape Cod, expect ticks. If you like the feel of sweat dropping off your brow and dampening the small of your back, July and August are the months for you. September brings clear skies, still-warm days, and the end of bugs.

Physical Fitness

Hiking demands proper conditioning. The best equipment will not help you reach your goal if you are out of shape. Once on the trail and beyond the limits of civilzation you must depend upon your feet, legs, back, hands, and cardiovascular system. A fit body will insure both enjoyment and completion of your trip.

Most people, however, can be optimistic about attempting these hikes. If time is not a factor and you can go at your own pace (which we recommend), you should find them all within your reach. A few of the Class III hikes—plus those in Class IV—are strenuous though

and well-toned muscles will make a significant difference.

We believe that jogging provides the best all-around preparation for hiking. It strengthens not only the seventy-five percent of the body's muscles located in the lower back and below, but the heart and lungs as well. If extensive hiking is your objective, include some hills in your jogging. If you cannot jog, walking is an alternate—though less effective—preparatory exercise.

Clothing

Comfortable clothing for hiking is made of materials that allow a balance between ventilation and insulation. Insulation must prevent the loss of body heat. Ventilation is necessary to dissipate the water vapor released from the skin's pores.

Fit is important. Legs must be able to move, bend, and stretch freely with no binding or chafing. Arm movement, too, must be unrestricted. Shorts that are roomy around the thighs are by far our favorites for warm weather. A day hike up a mountain requires packing

longer pants because of unpredictable temperature changes at higher elevations. Wide-legged, lightweight rainpants will keep you warm and dry and pull on easily over boots.

Cotton T shirts breathe well, are lightweight, and feel good next to the skin (fishnet T shirts are quite popular, although more expensive). Cotton chamois shirts provide good button-over warmth and, at sixteen ounces, are a weight bargain. The hooded parka from a rain-suit can serve as either wet-gear or windbreaker.

The cold and snow which can occur in Massachusetts from late fall through late spring demand specially-designed clothing. Garments which provide maximum warmth at minimum weight are vital for survival and comfort when hiking in cold, windy conditions.

Carefully-chosen footwear can cushion the foot over rough terrain, protect ankles from twisting and spraining, and provide a reasonable degree of

Chesterfield Gorge

warmth and water repellency. City footwear is generally useless, even potentially dangerous. For all the aforementioned reasons, we recommend hiking boots. Medium-weight ones (three pounds) are adequate for all the hikes in this book. Lug soles are durable, flexible, and grip well. Boot uppers and seams need to be treated with oil, grease, wax, or silicone. Socks provide insulation, help cushion the feet, and absorb perspiration and friction between boot and foot. A heavy wool sock fitted over a lighter inner one is a comfortable and practical combination. Wool, even if it gets wet, will keep your feet warm.

Food

Keeping food light is important on day hikes as well as backpacking trips. Cans add both weight and bulk. Fresh foods might spoil or melt.

Many companies produce large varieties of freeze-dried foods which are ideal for the backpacker. Light in weight and surprisingly tasty, they are a convenience for the day hiker too. Whatever your tastes, you

can satisfy them with freeze-dried meats, eggs, vegetables, soups, desserts, or fruits. Many of these foods are ready to eat after adding water (either hot or cold) eliminating the need to spend extra time preparing meals. The packages can also be easily tucked into a litter bag for the return trip.

For an energy treat you might consider cheese rather than chocolate. Cheeses have a high energy output; the drier ones are best. Romano, Parmesan, Provolone, and Kasseri are the driest. But Swiss and Cheddar have a water content too high to be recommended. Because of its high fat content (more than fifty percent in unsweetened varieties) chocolate is much harder to digest than other candy. Eating large amounts of it just before or during strenuous activity often produces an upset stomach instead of a spurt of energy.

The romantic, blazing wood-fire must become an anachronism. Downed wood is an increasingly scarce commodity and fire presents a constant danger to woodlands and wildlife. A variety of gas-fueled, compact stoves are readily available and preferable for the use of hikers.

First Aid and Survival

The best medicine is prevention. Become familiar with what lies ahead, bring suitable supplies, and know what to do in an emergency.

Brush up on first-aid procedures and bring a first-aid kit with you. (We include a snakebite kit in ours. See "Flora and Fauna.") Have a compass and map and know how to use them. (In Massachusetts the compass points about thirteen degrees west of north.) Take a flashlight and extra batteries—just in case. If you do become lost or injured—don't panic. Remain calm, assess your situation, and act according to your knowledge of the area.

Flora and Fauna

Throughout this book we have passed on information which will aid in the identification of trees, shrubs, flowers, and animals you may see.

Mammals, birds, reptiles,

amphibians, and fish (and some insects) can often be recognized by their "signs." Such signs include tracks, droppings, nests, burrows, dams, gnawings, rubbings, and scratchings. To the careful observer, they can indicate an animal's search for food, a battle, a slow or fast passage, perhaps even its age.

Keen senses enable wild animals to flee or take cover at your approach. They will not attack unless they feel threatened (especially if cornered) or fear for the safety of their young. This is also true of the two poisonous snakes in Massachusetts, the copperhead and timber rattlesnake. These snakes have been seen in the Blue Hills Reservation, the Mount Tom Reservation, the Holyoke Range, and in the Berkshires south of Great Barrington. Nocturnal creatures, they find daytime hideaways in rocky crevices or camouflage themselves amidst piles of twigs and leaves. They may also be found sunning on exposed rocks. To avoid unintentionally disturbing one of these pit vipers, use special care when hiking in these

areas. Watch where you place your hands and feet. Thousands of people hike the trails in these areas without ever seeing a poisonous snake. But we recommend carrying a snakebite kit, just in case.

Leaves, bark, flowers, fruit, buds, fragrance, color, and dimensions are clues used in the identification of trees, shrubs, and flowers. Help protect the forests by leaving all plant life as you find it.

Preserving Our Heritage

Some guidelines for insuring that what we enjoy today will be there for others to enjoy tomorrow:
Keep your group small.
Carry out empty what you carried in full.
Pick up the litter of less thoughtful persons.
Don't contaminate water.
Bury body waste if sanitary facilities are not available.
Burn burnables only if a fire is permitted.
Do not cut trees or branches.
Leave no sign of your presence.

SOME ADDRESSES TO KNOW
ABOUT

Appalachian Mountain Club
5 Joy Street
Boston, Massachusetts 02108

Massachusetts Audubon Society
Route 117
Lincoln, Massachusetts 01773

Trustees of Reservations
224 Adams Street
Milton, Massachusetts 02186

U.S. Department of the Interior
National Park Service
Washington, D.C. 20242

United State Geological Survey
Washington, D.C. 20242

Eastern Massachusetts

Cape Cod Sand Dunes

1. Beech Forest Trail

Class: I
Distance (around loop): 1 mile
Hiking Time: ½ hour

The Cape Cod National Seashore preserves both the natural and historic features of the area. You can mix camping, swimming, hiking, cycling, surfing, and horseback riding with exploration of historic buildings, sites, and markers. Twenty-seven thousand acres of land will eventually be available for the enjoyment of all who visit the Cape's easternmost stretches.

Shaded paths edged with lush greenery await you at the Beech Forest Trail in the Province Lands Area. Much of this gentle walk follows the outline of two freshwater ponds; the rest is a ramble through beautiful beech forests. Allow time to explore the short side paths which take you even closer to the varied natural features.

From US 6 in Provincetown, turn north at the traffic light on Race Point Road. Drive ½ mile to the Beech Forest Trail parking area on the left. (If you wish to purchase a guide pamphlet to the Beech Forest Trail, continue straight ahead to the Cape Cod National Seashore

Pitch Pine in Beech Forest

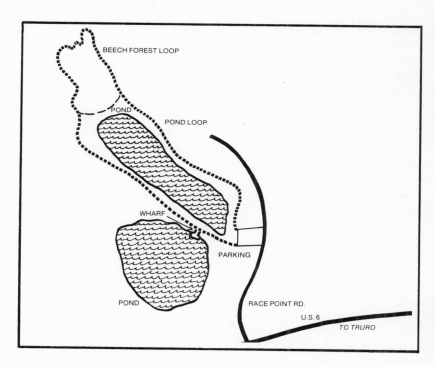

Province Lands Center.)

This northern tip of Cape Cod was once blanketed by thriving forests. Early settlers from Europe, however, gave little thought to preserving the natural resources. Clear cutting, overgrazing, and forest fires destroyed the native forests and meadows. Shifting dunes and blown sand threatened to eliminate the Province Lands settlements. In the 1800s strict conservation controls and beach grass plantings began to stabilize the movement of the dunes.

The Beech Forest Trail branches right from the end of the parking area. Wood chips surface the path. The way swings left and passes by beautiful clumps of wrinkled rose. Its distinctive characteristics are heavily wrinkled leaves and hairy stems. The large, deep, pink blossoms occasionally fade to

Beech Forest Trail

white. On long voyages colonial seamen consumed the wrinkled rose hips to prevent scurvy; today Cape Codders make jelly from them.

Trees and shrubs hug the way as you pass a pond and cross a small wooden footbridge. Short side trails invite you to explore the pond's edges. If you step quietly, you'll be greeted by bulging eyes and croaking voices. With further searching you may sight basking turtles, ducks, and wading birds. Look still closer for the movements of water striders, dragonflies, and whirligig beetles.

The footing along the main trail becomes softer as the sand deepens.

Several different species of pine fill the woods. You can identify pitch pine by its needles (in bunches of three) and dead cones still on the branches. Scotch pine has rust-colored bark and two short, twisted needles (one-half to three inches long) per bundle. Austrian pine has longer needles (up to six inches) also grouped in twos.

Oaks mingle with the pines as the trail eases past rising sand hills and reaches a fork. The left path continues around the pond. Go right for a pleasant walk through the beech forest. These handsome trees have smooth, steel-grey bark and prominently toothed elliptical leaves.

After approximately ½ mile the way swings sharply left and climbs a sandy embankment. Logs cross the trail forming a series of rustic steps.

The path labors downward over more steps and winds past dunes to the other side of the pond. Shadows in the sand reflect the needled branches above.

Pond lilies almost smother the watery surface to the left. In late spring and summer their thick yellow flowers become erect and bloom atop the large, protective leaves.

Ahead to the right a plank wharf extends into a smaller pond. Here you can linger in the sun and enjoy the isolated beauty. Animal and wind sounds keep you company.

Return to the parking area the way you came.

Beech Forest Trail

2.   Wellfleet Bay Wildlife Sanctuary

Class: I
Distance (round trip): 1.5 miles
Hiking time: 1 hour

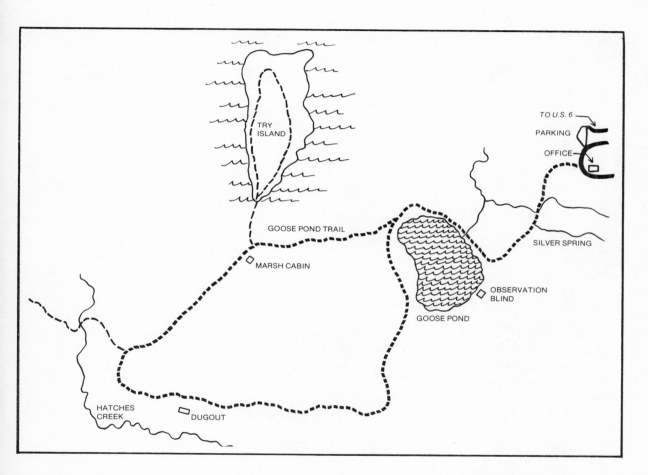

Until the British blockade during the Revolutionary War ruined their economy, Wellfleet settlers reaped wealth from the sea through whaling and oystering. Desperate bartering with England and France restored the town's prosperity until the Embargo Act of 1807 halted trade once again. By 1850, however, only Gloucester surpassed Wellfleet in cod and mackerel catches. The Wellfleet oyster beds were the richest in New England. Today that era has passed and tourism provides the town with most of its income.

The Wellfleet Bay Wildlife Sanctuary offers an opportunity

Wellfleet Bay Wildlife Sanctuary

Bullfrog

to explore the area's natural history. The Massachusetts Audubon Society purchased the 350-acre Austin Ornithological Research Station in 1958. That original parcel and a more recently acquired 350 acres comprise the pine woods, moorland, and saltmarsh of the present wildlife sanctuary. It is one of the largest private bird banding stations in the world.

Shortly after you cross from Eastham into Wellfleet on US 6, watch for the blue and white Massachusetts Audubon Society sign on the left. Turn in and follow signs to the sanctuary. There is an admission charge for those not members of the society: $2 per car, $1 per bicycle or motorcycle, $1 per pedestrian, and $20 per bus.

From the parking area walk around to the left to the sign for the Goose Pond Trail. (At the office in the building to the left, you may purchase Goose Pond Trail booklets which detail the seventy-one stations

Wellfleet Bay Wildlife Sanctuary

along this self-guiding nature trail.)

Soon after beginning your walk you'll pass Silver Spring Brook on the left. A dam causes the brook to form a shallow pond which is gradually filling up with silt and plant debris. Side paths poke through pond-edge greenery allowing opportunities for glimpses of pond life.

A vista across marshlands to the ocean unfolds as you emerge from the pines. Wild lupine flourishes in the sandy soil at the trail edges. In has pea-like blue flowers and radiating leaves consisting of seven to ten segments.

The path approaches Goose Pond and swings right (a small structure for observing and photographing wildlife sets on the pond's left shore). Red-winged blackbirds abound in this marshland area. The red, yellow-bordered shoulder patch identifies the otherwise black male. Females resemble large sparrows with heavier streaking and longer bills. The promiscuous males may mate with several females in each breed-

ing season. Listen for the liquid *kong-ka-ree* call.

The way continues past Goose Pond over a wooden boardwalk. Bear right at the fork beyond the pond. As the main trail reaches a small cabin on the left, a secondary loop trail leads right to Try Island. At the time of the vernal and the autumnal equinox the tide inundates the entire marsh with the exception of this island.

Just ahead another side trail branches right and leads across a wooden footbridge over Hatches Creek to a beach. If you go in this direction, keep an eye on the time. Remember that high tide may flood the approaches to the footbridge.

Continuing its loop around to the left, the main trail passes a low, dugout structure on the right. Notice the many small bird houses along the way where tree swallows frequently nest. Completely white underneath, they are the only green-backed swallows commonly seen in the east. Their swooping aerial acrobatics and wide mouths aid them in capturing insects. In cold weather they feed on bay-

berries found in thickets on interior dunes.

Bayberries are actually wax-covered nutlets also enjoyed by wintering eastern bluebirds and yellow-rumped warblers. The waxy coating makes good candles. When crushed or baked in the sun, the leaves give off a pungent fragrance (bayberry's generic name, *Myrica,* comes from the Greek word for perfume).

The Goose Pond Trail completes its loop at the fork just west of Goose Pond. Turn right onto this familiar section of the trail and follow it back to the parking lot.

Wellfleet Bay Wildlife Sanctuary

3. Buttonbush Trail (braille trail)

Class: I
Distance (around loop): .25 miles
Hiking time: ½ hour

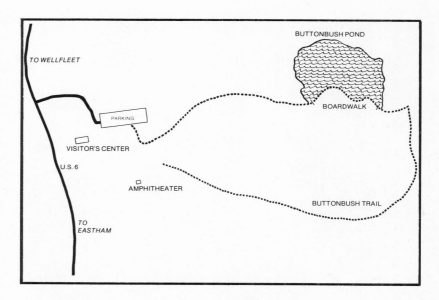

The Buttonbush Trail allows blind persons to enjoy the environment that the rest of us take so much for granted. Signposts with text in both braille and large print remind you to stop often to touch, listen, and smell. A guide rope runs alongside the three-foot-wide path. Pieces of garden hose around the rope warn you to step cautiously ahead, while two-inch plastic disks signal the presence of trail signs. For those gifted with sight, we suggest closing your eyes while walking this ¼-mile route.

The Buttonbush Trail loops through cool, shaded woodlands and skirts the edge of a fresh-water pond at the Cape Cod National Seashore's Salt Pond Center. From US 6 in North Eastham turn east into the large parking lot. The trail begins at the signpost next to the yellow guide rope below and to the left of the Salt Pond Visitors' Center.

The path itself offers contrasts in footing for those who notice. Your feet crunch over soft bits of shredded red cedar, re-

Approaching Buttonbush Pond

sound dully against a raised boardwalk, and pound jarringly onto hard-packed sand. Logs cross the trail intermittently, forming steps in sloping sections.

Sudden temperature changes dramatize your journey. The refreshing coolness of shaded trails abruptly turns to heat as you walk out into sun, only to return just as quickly to the comfort of shady paths.

Red cedar, pitch pine, and several other trees and shrubs await your tactile and olfactory

inspection. Listen for the sounds of pond life: the gurgling call of a red-winged blackbird or the sudden plop of a frog's leap to the protection of deeper water.

Automobile noises call attention to the proximity of Nauset Road, but will you know from the clicking of chains and gears or the soft whirring of tires that a bicycle path has begun to parallel the Buttonbush Trail?

The walk ends about 20 steps from where it began.

Blending human and natural history, the Fort Hill Trail visits the Captain Edward Penniman House, climbs Fort Hill, skirts Nauset Marsh, crosses Skiff Hill, and explores the Red Maple Swamp.

From the rotary junction of US 6, Mass 6A, and Mass 28 in Eastham, drive north on route 6 for 1.2 miles to the blue and white Cape Cod National Seashore-Fort Hill sign. Swing right onto Governor Prence Road. Turn right again onto Fort Hill Road and follow it a short way to the sign for parking on the left.

The Fort Hill Trail begins at the whalebone archway in front of the Penniman House. Building such gateways is a Cape Cod custom that dates back to prosperous whaling days.

Wellfleet shipwrights constructed the Captain Edward Penniman House in 1867 from plans which the Captain brought back from France. Being a prosperous whaleship captain, he wanted his nineteenth-century Victorian home to be the

Whalebone arches

Fort Hill Trail

4.   Fort Hill Trail

Class: II
Distance (round trip): 1.5 miles
Hiking time: 1¼ hours

most elegant in Eastham. However, history records that the equally elegant taxes on the grand house upset Captain Penniman who wrote: "My house is much overvalued and you value my horse and buggy at $100; you may have same by paying me $45."

The trail loops around the house to the right then swings left around the barn and descends into a hollow of locust trees. Drooping clusters of fragrant white flowers decorate the trees in spring.

The house to the left beyond the hollow is nearly 150 years old. It was constructed by the Knowles family who farmed land on Fort and Skiff hills.

Climb up the path to Fort Hill for a vista that includes Orleans Cove to the right, Nauset Marsh immediately before you, and the Atlantic beyond. Unfriendly Indians and the shallowness of Nauset Harbor thwarted Samuel de Champlain's attempt to establish a settlement here in 1605.

Walk across the parking lot atop Fort Hill and along the

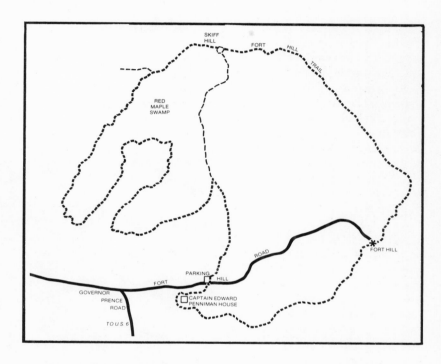

downward-sloping path to a large glacial boulder. Some say that early settlers used the spike driven into the south side of this great rock to anchor a pulley for hauling ashore loads of salt hay. Rich in nutrients, the hay was used as livestock food and bedding, or as a garden mulch. The ring implanted in another glacial boulder down on the beach was probably also used in harvesting salt hay.

Along the way to Skiff Hill look across Nauset Marsh for a possible glimpse of a great blue heron.

Cooling ocean breezes refresh your walk toward Skiff Hill. A maze of inlets and tidal creeks meander through the marshland below to the right. Song sparrows perch atop thickets of wrinkled roses and sing *Madge, Madge, Madge, pleeese put a kettle on.*

The trail curves through a young forest of eastern red cedar and pitch pine toward Skiff Hill. Atop the hill an open-sided, octagonal structure shelters Indian Rock. A Nauset Indian community used the boulder as a grinding rock, sharpening tools and weapons on its concave surfaces. They shaped bonepoints and fish hooks in the rock's narrow depressions.

From Skiff Hill, a shortcut leads left, back toward the parking lot. Go right, down the paved path to the trail which leads sharply left into the north end of the Red Maple Swamp. Go left onto this new trail. In the early morning or late afternoon you may see cottontail rabbits feeding in the grassy areas beside the paved trail.

Turn left at the sign for the Red Maple Swamp. Numerous weathered, gray boardwalks curl through the lush vegetation. Narrow, scaly plates shingle the massive hulks of aged red maples. Cinnamon fern and wood fern flourish.

Leaving the swamp, the trail passes through meadows dotted with pines and cedars. After climbing log-girdled steps, you reach a trail junction. Turn right for the short walk back to the parking area.

Lady's Slippers

Fort Hill Trail

5. Yarmouth Botanic Trails

Class: I
Distance: 1.25 miles
Hiking time: ¾ hour

A wheel-shaped herb garden introduces you to the Yarmouth Botanic Trails. Rosemary (signifying remembrance) rises from the center: each herb in the garden (the property of the Historical Society of Old Yarmouth) is in memory of a former patron.

Indians originally called this area Mattacheset, meaning "old or planting lands by the borders of the water." Here they planted beans, pumpkins, and corn in natural and man-made clearings. Deer and smaller game filled the forests while ponds provided habitats for fish and waterfowl. There is little wonder that this naturally rich region was one of the first to be appropriated by the white men.

Anthony Thatcher, one of the three founders of Yarmouth, selected 156 acres of the best land for himself. He eventually paid the Indians with coats, breeches, hoes, hatchets, and metal kettles. Though Thatcher descendants distinguished themselves in both the town and the outside world, they retained a love for the original land. A few years ago a Thatcher relative

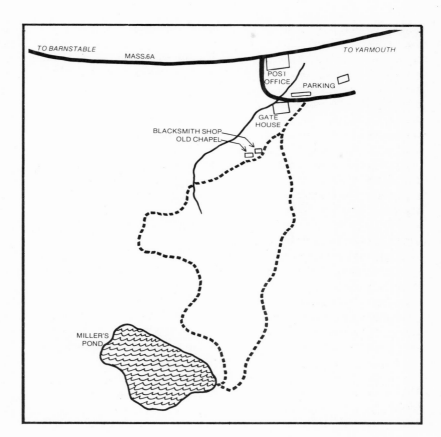

generously donated the present fifty-acre tract to the historical society.

To reach the start of this hike turn south from Mass 6A onto the dirt road leading behind the Yarmouth Port Post Office. Drive the short distance to the

parking area near the gate house. A charge of 50¢ for adults and 25¢ for children covers the cost of admission and a pamphlet describing the route.

The sandy trail begins to the left of the wheel of thyme. It

Yarmouth Botanic Trails

quickly branches left and follows a grassy swath cut through open fields. The way leads into a quiet area forested with pitch pine, the Cape's most common pine. It generally grows on poor soils and can withstand strong winds and salt spray.

Oaks begin to mix with the pines. Delicate, pink lady's slippers dot the trail sides at ground level. A member of the orchid family, the flower can be easily identified by the singular, puffed-out, pink petal resembling the toe of a slipper. Two oval leaves from six to eight inches long grow from the base of the stalk. Each plant has only one flower and one stem. Laws prohibit the picking of these flowers.

The stillness of the young oak forest might be broken by rustlings in the leaves; possibly from a chipmunk or squirrel, but more probably from a rufous-sided towhee. Its unmistakable call is a slurred *chewink*. The large size (up to eight inches), dark heads, rusty sides, white bellies, and large white spots at the corners of the long, rounded tails make them easily identifiable. Towhees feed almost exclusively on the ground, persistently scratching away dead leaves to get at the insects underneath.

Step down over the log-supported stairway to Miller's Pond. A short spur takes you to the water's edge. You may see animal tracks as well as frogs and turtles from this tiny observation area. Migrating waterfowl feed here in spring and fall.

Return to the main trail and follow it along the northern shore. Pine odors engulf you as you weave your way through open fields. Cross the heavy board footbridge and feel the crisp crunch of woodchips underfoot. Upon arriving at the old chapel and black-smith shop, look right to the top of the hill. A massive purple beech dominates the skyline. Behind it is the skeletal shape of a rare Japanese geisha tree.

The path swings right and leads back to the parking area.

Rosa Rugosa

Gus Ben David and American Kestrel

Plan to spend several enjoyable and informative hours at the Felix Neck Wildlife Sanctuary on Martha's Vineyard. Interpretive pamphlets guide you over miles of trails through open fields and woodlands, and along marshes, beaches, and small ponds. (This hike is just a sample of what is there.) An observation house enables you to watch and identify a living collection of native waterfowl. From a photography blind you can gaze at or take pictures of wild waterfowl. The visitors' center provides maps, booklets, exhibits, and a library with a good ecological and environmental reference collection. Knowledgeable staff and volunteers stand ready to answer your questions.

In 1963 George Moffett became the owner of the 200 acres that now make up the sanctuary. At that time he knew only that he wanted the land to be used for conservation. He and two close friends gathered a group of interested people to develop a program and an organization. A nature

Felix Neck Wildlife Sanctuary

6. Felix Neck Wildlife Sanctuary

Class: I
Distance (round trip): 1.75 miles
Hiking time: 1½ hours

awareness program for children began under the auspices of the Martha's Vineyard Natural Historical Society in 1964.

In 1967 the land was donated to the Massachusetts Audubon Society with the understanding that the program would be administered by the Felix Neck Wildlife Trust (the offspring of the Martha's Vineyard Natural Historical Society). The Audubon Society holds title to the land and the Trust operates and financially supports the sanctuary program. A collection box beneath a sign reading "Your donations keep us growing" reflects the unique atmosphere of this program.

Under sanctuary manager Gus Ben David II, research on rehabilitating sick and injured birds began in 1970. One of Gus' prime interests is working with birds of prey. He has an injured snowy owl, an American kestrel, a golden eagle, and an abused bald eagle under rehabilitative treatment.

Ferries from Woods Hole, Falmouth Heights (summer only), and Hyannis (summer only) will get you to Martha's Vineyard.

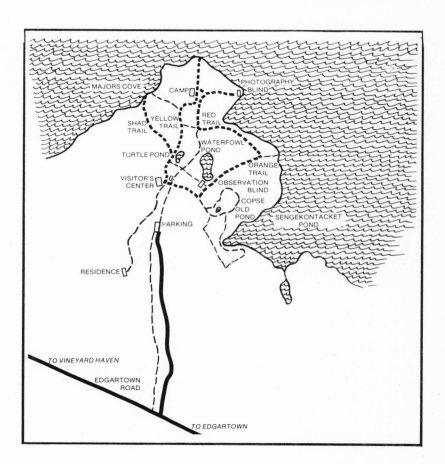

From Vineyard Haven, proceed south 4 miles on Edgartown Road. An attractive sign marks the entrance to the Felix Neck Wildlife Sanctuary on the left. Follow the narrow, sandy access road almost 1 mile to the parking area.

From the far end of the parking lot walk through the trees to the visitors' center. You may see ring-necked pheasants and bobwhites scurrying around this area. They are tame enough to let you have a close look, but wary enough to know when to strut away.

You'll want to browse through the center before tackling the trails. When ready to stretch your legs, walk left around the donation box ("Your donations keep us growing") to the Yellow Trail markers.

The flat grassy path passes an open field and winds through a narrow wooded area. Rising onto walkalongs, it reaches a small semicircular pond. The Shad Trail exits left here and is lined with blueberry bushes. Follow it through cool woods to a small marshy strip at the edge of Major's Cove.

Return to the Yellow Trail and follow it left through older, thicker woods. The alternately sandy and grassy path weaves in and out of wooded areas before arriving at a small weathered building. This structure is primarily used as a study and research facility, but doubles during bad weather as a classroom for the summer camp program.

The Yellow Trail passes by the camp and slithers between high-bush blueberries. Poison ivy grows throughout this area and serves as a constant reminder to remain on the trails. At the end of the Yellow Trail you look across Major's Cove to the sandy finger of Edgartown Beach.

Retrace your steps to the camp and take the trail to the photography blind which exits left from the circular road in front of the camp. Whether you have a camera or not, the small wooden shelter offers an ideal spot from which to observe wild waterfowl on Sengekontacket Pond, especially in winter.

Swing left back at the circular road and follow it to the Red Trail. Keep an eye out for white-tailed deer tracks in the sand, their two-toed hooves leave cleft, heart-shaped prints.

Turn left onto the Red Trail. Fresh sea breezes will cool your face as you walk out to the shores of Sengekontacket Pond again. Try whistling *bob white* to the quail which enliven this area.

A right turn onto the Orange Trail takes you to the observation blind at the edge of Waterfowl Pond. Here you can watch the flocks of native dabbling and diving ducks. Because the sanctuary is located on a migratory flyway and because the many types of captive waterfowl act as decoys, numerous species of wild waterfowl visit the pond each year.

Follow the Orange Trail back to the visitors' center. Remember there are other trails still awaiting your exploration within the sanctuary.

Felix Neck Wildlife Sanctuary

7.   Ashumet Holly Reservation

Class: I
Distance (around reservation): 1.25 miles
Hiking time: 1 hour

The late Wilfred Wheeler donated his forty-five acre Ashumet Farm to the Massachusetts Audubon Society so that his unique holly collection gathered from all over the Cape and its islands would be preserved. From some of the older American holly trees still growing in the reservation, he developed winter-hardy strains. Varieties of European and Oriental hollies and other native plants also grow here. The twigs, berries, and bark of hollies provide food for area wildlife.

From the intersection of Mass 151 and Mass 28 in North Falmouth, drive east on route 151 for 4 miles. The Ashumet Holly Reservation is on the north side of the road in East Falmouth. Signs direct you to the reservation and the small parking area across from the barn.

The voluntary admission charge is $1 per car. A small information center in the barn sells 25¢ guides to the sixty numbered stations along the reservation's trails.

Walk beside a row of pines left of the barn to a tiny clearing.

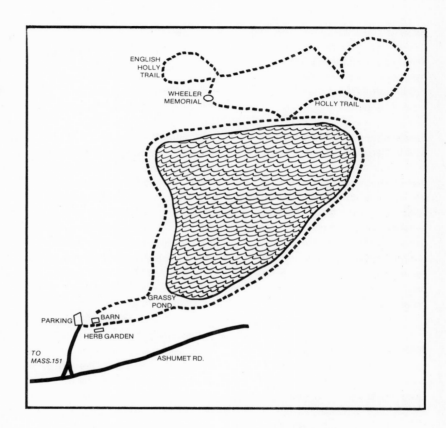

Before you grows a small group of heathers and heaths. Follow the light blue triangles left down the hill toward Grassy Pond.

The path continues parallel to, but above, the water. At a trail junction a blue marker points left. Go right toward the pond's edge and cross over the ramp. Moccasin flower or pink lady's slipper grows abundantly here. Dense cover near the pond provides a habitat favored by gray catbirds. Mewing calls punctuate their squeaky song.

Continue along the shore to the

Ashumet Holly Reservation

second trail leading left (marked by a green and white Holly Trail sign) and take it. The numbered stations identified in the Holly Trail pamphlet begin just before this turn.

In late spring you may surprise a ruffed grouse in lush growth at the trail's edge. If accompanied by chicks, the hen will go into her broken wing act to entice you away from her family. With wing dragging, she'll draw attention to herself and cunningly lead you away from the young. When the danger is past, she'll thunder into the air and return to the chicks.

Beige markers guide you through an evergreen forest past the start of the Crater Loop Trail (on the right). Bear left at the fork ahead, following the consecutively numbered stations. Turn left at the T intersection. Walk to station 28 on the left, then retrace your steps to the junction and continue past a bench on your left. Swing sharply right at station 30 which identifies franklinia. In 1790 John Bartram discovered the last wild franklinia along the

Altamaha River in Georgia. This unusual shrub flowers in the fall.

At a four-trail intersection ahead go left past the Heather Horseshoe on the right. Bear right at the fork ahead (past station 35). The trees in the nursery to the left at station 38 include members of the magnolia, heath, and dogwood families.

At the intersection near station 40 branch right onto the English Holly Trail. Bear left at the next intersection and left again onto an old road and return to the start of the English Holly Trail.

Go sharply right past station 41 and turn left, guided by a trail sign, into a clearing. An assortment of holly trees ring the open area. To the left is the Wheeler Memorial. A bench here (one of the many throughout the reservation) encourages you to pause and relax.

Take the path to the right of the memorial stone. This route parallels the Pond Trail (below to the right) and joins with it a short distance ahead. Step down to the Pond Trail and go left for the return trip around the water.

A glimpse of pond life will reward your careful observations. The semiaquatic ribbon snake frequents the muddy shore during dry weather. In the shallows, black bullheads, commonly called catfish, wriggle in search of food among underwater plant stems. Belted kingfishers chatter from their perches in pine branches overhanging the water.

Remain on the Pond Trail until you reach the trail intersection where a sign directs you left to the barn. Walk through the herb garden and back to the parking area.

Holly

Ashumet Holly Reservation

8.   Myles Standish State Forest

Class: I
Distance (round trip): 2.25 miles
Hiking time: 1¼ hours

Pilgrim and Puritan histories cite Captain Myles Standish, for whom this forest was named, as the man who restored moral sobriety to the Massachusetts Bay Colony by deporting Thomas Morton. Morton, who traded rum and firearms to the Indians for furs, established a settlement at Mount Wollaston (rechristened Merry Mount) in 1625. The uninhibited carryings-on he encouraged in the people, coupled with the financially important fact that his trade cut into the Plymouth settlement's earnings, moved Governor William Bradford to have the Merry Mount founder castigated. In 1628 Captain Myles Standish arrested Thomas Morton and banished him to England. (In 1637, Morton wrote the book *Newe English Canaan,* in which he bitingly attacked the Pilgrims' and Puritans' moral hypocrisy.)

You reach the Myles Standish State Forest, located in Carver and Plymouth, by following signs from US 3 in Plymouth or Mass 58 in South Carver. Approaching the forest from route 58, you'll pass acres of

Pond reflections

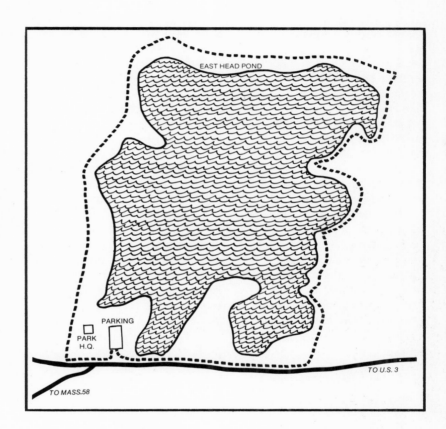

cranberry bogs alongside the road. Carver claims the distinction of being the cranberry center of the world.

The cranberry's pale pink blossoms and protruding, red and yellow, beaklike stamens were thought to resemble a crane. Thus the fruit's original

name: crane berry. Indians colored rugs and blankets with cranberry juice and flavored pemmican cakes and succotash with its tartness. Pilgrim women used the native fruit in cooking and cheered their wardrobes with the crimson pigment. Both Indians and the early settlers believed in the fruit's

Myles Standish State Forest

healing powers. Pequod Indians of Cape Cod treated poison arrow wounds with a cranberry poultice. They also imbibed the juice to calm their nerves. Rich in vitamin C, cranberries helped prevent scurvy among early American seamen voyaging to distant ports.

Leave your car in the parking area beside the comfort station (park headquarters). Walk left from the parking area on the blacktop road for about ¼ mile. Beyond the bicycle crossing (two parallel white lines crossing the road), you'll see a blue triangle on the left. Turn into the woods and follow the trail across the blacktop bicycle path and onto an old wooded road.

As you follow this eastern shore of the pond, note the predominate type of pine bordering the trail. The pitch pine's stiff, yellow-green needles are grouped in threes. These ragged-looking trees have short, spindly branches protruding from their twisted trunks.

Knee-level greenery includes blueberry bushes, ferns, and young oaks. At ankle height you may spy wild lily of the valley, also called Canada mayflower. Wild birds feast on its maroon-freckled, pale red berries.

When the old road bears sharply right, follow the path straight ahead. Blue triangles guide you. Occasional spurs to the left invite you to explore the shore further. Alert eyes will glimpse the swollen, pink, purple-veined petals of moccasin flowers growing near the trail.

After 1 mile of hiking, turn left as the trail meets a wide, sandy road at right angles. Go left again onto the blacktop road a short distance ahead. Blue triangles guide you along this road, then left at a distant fork.

Sun-loving common buttercups highlight the roadsides. Cows and other grass-eating animals do not eat the buttercup's poorly

flavored leaves and stems, which may explain why it abounds.

You'll follow the hard-surface road for approximately ¾ mile. One hundred yards beyond the parallel white lines of a bicycle crossing, swing left into the woods at the blue triangle. Go straight across the gravel road intersecting from the left.

Soon the trail joins the hard-packed gravel road it has been paralleling on the left. A lovely stand of eastern white pine fills the gentle slope above to the right. Largest of the Northeast conifers, these giants thrust their whorled heads seventy-five to one hundred feet into the air.

Blue triangles mark the way on the now-sandy road. Cross the blacktop bicycle path and proceed to the paved road. Turn left toward the parking lot.

9. World's End

Class: II
Distance (round trip): 2.75 miles
Hiking time: 1½ hours

World's End is "an island of beauty where we can still enjoy the satisfaction of lying in a field of warm grass and looking at the sky; where we can still watch wildlife undisturbed by the noise and confusion of the city; where we can still walk on beaches washed by the sea without seawalls and hotdog concessions; and where we can turn momentarily to simple pleasures such as seeing a child explore the mysteries of the coming spring."*

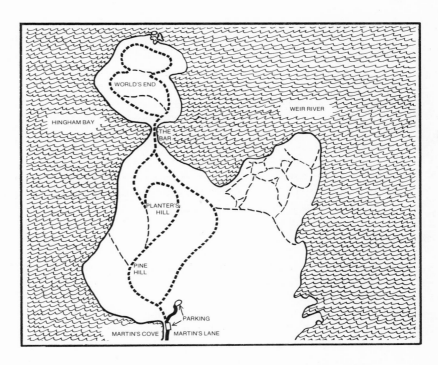

Only 14 miles from downtown Boston, World's End lies surrounded by water on all sides except the south. Shady lanes stretch leisurely along open meadowlands throughout this inviting peninsula. The area was never developed or industrialized. During the nineteenth and early twentieth centuries local farms used it for pasture, hay meadows, and cropland. To save it from subdivision by developers, members of the Committee to Preserve World's End raised $450,000, purchased

*Letter from Samuel Wakeman, as chairman of the Committee to Preserve World's End.

the land in 1967, and donated it to the Trustees of Reservations.

You are welcome to enjoy the area at your own pace, but picnic lunches are not allowed. The main gate remains open from 10 a.m. to 5 p.m.; a fee of 50¢ admits everyone fifteen years of age and older (under fifteen, free).

Approach the Summer Street traffic circle in East Hingham on Mass 3A from either the northwest or south. Leave route 3A and follow the road going east from the circle to the first traffic light. Turn left onto Martin's Lane. Drive ¾ mile to the sign for World's End and go right. Six cars may park in the small lot just before the entrance (no parking is allowed on streets in this area); additional parking space is available beyond the chain gate.

Bear left from the entrance on the wide gravel road. Old, heavy oaks and maples line the way. Stay straight at the fork ahead and continue up the incline of Pine Hill. At its crest striking views to the west unfold before you. Tree-covered, rocky islands rise from the waters of Martin's Cove and Hingham Bay. The Boston skyline looms to the north.

In summer a wide variety of saltwater recreationists enjoy themselves below. Surfcasters heave lures out into the coastal waters in hopes of claiming prized striped bass. Boaters ply the protected bay in everything from dinghies to sleek ketches and yawls. Swimmers splash in the sun-warmed cove.

Staying straight on the grassier of the two routes at the next fork leads you up the east side of Planter's Hill. To the right you can see the humpbacked roller coaster at Nantasket Beach's Paragon Park with the Atlantic beyond. Thick, ankle-high grass swishes against shoes as you circle to the left for a better view of the Boston

skyline. Wildflowers dot the open fields stretching beyond the tree-lined path. Yellow king devils and red-orange devil's paintbrush dab the landscape with color. Both have numerous blossoms sitting atop hairy stems.

When back at the main trail turn sharply right and follow the gravel-filled path down to the narrow neck of land known as the Bar. (If the tide is out, you'll smell the mudflats long before reaching this area.) This causeway connecting the outermost two hills with the mainland was built by early settlers to bear traffic during high tides.

Bypass two trails leading left from the main path and wind along the eastern route of World's End. Salt breezes brush the tops of tufted meadow grass and enliven your senses with ocean sounds and smells.

Bearing right at a T intersection you suddenly find low shrubs lining the way with staghorn sumac predominating.

Horsechestnut trees border

the path ahead. Native to Asia and southeastern Europe, they are planted as shade and street trees in the United States.

The high-grassed fields provide an ideal habitat for upland game birds. Bobwhites will rise from trailsides on almost soundless wings, but the more elusive ring-necked pheasant is harder to locate. These wary birds often prefer to run or hunker down in the grass to avoid detection. Pheasants fly powerfully, but only for brief distances on their short wings.

Completing the swing of the tip of World's End, stay right at the two forks ahead. You walk under the overhanging branches of thick-muscled American beeches and pass fields filled with ox-eye daisies.

Cross back over the bar and follow the left fork up the long, gradual slope. If you have the time, you could go left at the next fork and explore the network of trails traversing Rocky Neck. Whether you decide to go further or head back, your return route goes right at the fork and soon returns to the parking area.

World's End

Wild flowers

World's End

The Braintree Town Forest lies tucked away in the southernmost section of the town formerly called *Monoticut,* or "abundant," by the Massachusetts Indians. Discovering this woodland, amidst the suburban sprawl of a Greater Boston community produces both surprise and pleasure. Chosen from the numerous trails winding through the Braintree and adjoining Holbrook town forests, the Twin Forest and Cranberry Pond Loop Trails combine to take you on an attractive walk.

Reach the start of the Twin Forest Trail by driving south from South Braintree center about 1 mile on Mass 37. On the left, just beyond the corner of Peach Street and route 37, you'll see the sign for Braintree Town Forest. Turn left onto the dirt road and bear right to a wooded road exiting left. Park in the small area on the left.

Hike down the road between rows of eastern white pine and go left when you reach a fork in a small open area. Con-

Spider web

Braintree Town Forest

10. Braintree Town Forest

Class: II
Distance (round trip): 4 miles
Hiking time: 2¼ hours

tinuing along the flat, curving path, you soon reach a small campsite. Bear left and follow the trail marked with yellow blazes. The way, now uneven and rocky, begins to narrow.

A loud, sharp, ground-level *chock-chock-chock,* usually from the cover of brush or a tree stump vantage point, signals the presence of the sprightly eastern chipmunk.

Branch right at the next fork in the trail (huge chunks of rock pile along the right side of the path here) and left at the following one. Approximately 50 feet beyond, at still another fork, bear sharply left between low bushes closely edging the trail.

Go left at the T intersection and walk out of the woods onto a blacktop road. Continue straight to where this road meets Liberty Street. Turn right onto Liberty Street and then quickly left at a fork. Stay on this hardtop road to a left turn onto Braemore Road. After approximately 100 yards, turn sharply left onto a dirt road. At its end, branch left across a small wooden bridge over Cranberry Brook.

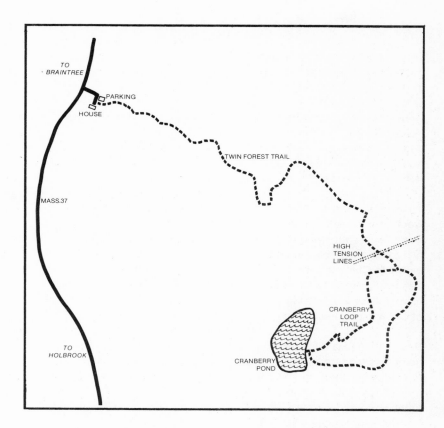

Climbing a slight rise, the trail forks again. Bear right past a hulking, whale-sized ledge. Hike through a stone wall and past a yellow-blazed trail on the right. Three hundred feet beyond, more yellow blazes mark an abrupt turn to the right. Take this hard-packed dirt trail to the open area beneath high tension lines.

In the thick greenery to the sides of the trail, note the pink, cuplike flowers of sheep laurel. The flowers of this heath family member cluster together at the drooping top of last year's growth of leaves. New leaves sprout above the clump of blossoms.

Cross beneath the high tension lines. At the intersection ahead, the Twin Forest Trail turns sharply left. Go right onto the Cranberry Pond Loop Trail. Yellow blazes mark this path and guide you right, near the high tension wire towers, then left into the woods.

Weaving through the hardwood forest, the Cranberry Pond Loop Trail swings sharply right as a blue-blazed trail exits left. Climb the short spur trail leading right to a small rocky hill for a limited view of Cranberry Pond beyond.

Return to the main trail and go right, swinging around below the rocky hill, then back to the left, following the trail down to the shore of Cranberry Pond. The large, floppy leaves of yellow pond lilies or spatterdock float in the shallows. Near shore in the summer, you can watch the spawning activities of the green sunfish. The males of this species push aside pond bottom vegetation and fan shallow depressions in the sand with their fins.

Retrace your steps back from the pond and bear right at the yellow marker (don't go back up the hill to the rocky mound). Almost immediately, the trail forks again; keep right along the lower path. This unmarked but well-cleared trail winds easterly away from Cranberry Pond. Swing left at the fork ahead and climb easily through blueberry bushes.

The Cranberry Pond Loop Trail rejoins the Twin Forest Trail at a T intersection. Go left, following the path past the blue-blazed trail entering from the left rear. Just ahead, you reach the opening where the power lines cross. Make a sharp left onto a narrow path (still the Twin Forest Trail). Follow this path along the southern side of the opening to the intersection where the Cranberry Pond Loop Trail starts. Turn right and retrace your route on the Twin Forest Trail to your car.

11. Great Blue Hill

Class: III
Elevation: 635 feet
Vertical rise: 983 feet
Distance (round trip): 3.5 miles
Hiking time: 2¼ hours

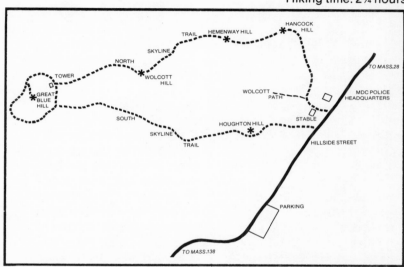

Only 15 miles south of Boston, the network of trails in the Blue Hills Reservation takes you over rocky terrain and through intriguing rock formations to panoramic overlooks. The trails forming your circular route to Great Blue Hill also include climbs over the summits of Houghton, Wolcott, Hemenway, and Hancock hills. Ascents of these additional peaks account for this hike's vertical rise being greater than the elevation of Great Blue Hill itself. To prevent twisted or sprained ankles on the rocky paths, it would be wise to wear hiking boots.

To reach the start of the South Skyline Trail, go north on Mass 138 from the intersection of Mass 128 and route 138 in Canton. Take the first right onto Blue Hill Street (it becomes Hillside Street). Follow this road for 1 mile and leave your car in the large parking area on the right.

Cross Hillside Street and walk right, watching for the blue-blazed, wooden signpost marking the start of the South Sky-

line Trail. Turn left and enter the woods. This first strenuous stretch rises steeply over a rocky trail. Trees spread talonlike roots across the path.

Along the way, recognize the quaking aspen by its circular, seeming-to-shiver leaves and smooth, greenish white bark. Its foliage quakes appropriately in the gentlest breeze.

Go left onto the graveled bridle path circling 435-foot high Houghton Hill, then left again at the blue blazes atop

a small, rocky hill. Look ahead to the summit of Great Blue Hill.

After a moderate descent, the South Skyline Trail crosses Houghton Path. It rises slightly over a knoll and descends again through white pine-filled woods before passing over Coon Hollow Brook. Ascend the slope beyond the brook and cross Coon Hollow Path.

Paralleling a brook to the left, the trail swings right and passes between massive boulders. A blue blaze on a large

Great Blue Hill

boulder ahead marks the crossing of the brook.

After passing over grassy Wildcat Notch Path, the final ¼ mile of the South Skyline Trail climbs up over open ledges with continuing views back to the south.

The trail meets the Eliot Circle Path after 1¼ miles. Walk left on this graveled route and survey the panorama stretching southeast and south. Ponkapog Pond is the large body of water directly below; Reservoir Pond lies to the west.

About halfway around this circuit route, the Summit Path, a macadam road, crosses the way. Turn right and walk up to the summit and weather observatory. Dr. Charles Brooks, considered the father of present-day meteorology, directed the Blue Hill Observatory for many years. He developed many of the sophisticated techniques used for recording and forecasting weather conditions.

Return to the Eliot Circle Path

South Skyline Trail

and go right to the stone observation tower. Long openings at the top of the tower allow you to enjoy views from northwest to southwest. The skyscrapers of Boston's skyline rise to the north. A bit east, islands dot the waters of Boston Harbor and Quincy Bay. Rolling hilltops complete the scene.

A blue-blazed, wooden post marks the start of the North Skyline Trail at the observation tower's base (just before the Eliot Bridge). Watch your step down this rocky path.

The sharp *clonk, clonk* of frogs reveals the presence of a pond to the right and marks the crossing of two trails. Walk across the first (Coon Hollow Path) and turn left onto the second (Wildcat Notch Path). Stay on it for 50 feet before turning right back onto the North Skyline Trail at the blue blazes. Swing right through a low, boggy area and up a narrow gouge to the summit of 470-foot Wolcott Hill.

Frogs croak through trees to the left as you drop down into a hollow and bear right. After

climbing a small ridge, the trail narrows between blueberry bushes and descends to the junction with Five Corner Path (a green police signal box stands to the left). Hike straight across this junction and follow the trail up the hill on the other side.

After mounting jagged ledge, stretch out on the top of Hemenway Hill (480 feet) for a few moments rest. The summit of Great Blue Hill rises in the distance. Bear right off the hill and swing sharply right at an arrow on the ledge. Step down to and cut across Break Neck Ledge Path.

Climb steeply again to a ridgeline, across the Circle Path, and on to the top of Hancock Hill (510 feet). Begin your descent on the narrow, grassy, blue-blazed path.

The North Skyline Trail descends steeply to meet broad Wolcott Path. Follow it left between the police barracks and horse barn to Hillside Street. Go right along the highway and return to the parking lot.

12. Stony Brook Nature Center

Class: I
Distance (round trip): 1 mile
Hiking time: ½ hour

This relaxing walk winds through quiet woods and around marshes and ponds. Along the Stony Brook Nature Trail you're apt to see migratory ducks and geese feeding, turtles sunning on tiny mud hummocks, chipmunks scurrying across shaded paths, frogs sitting bubble-eyed below the water's surface, or perhaps a great blue heron stalking fish in the shallows.

Drive south from the center of Norfolk on Mass 115 (Pond Street) for 1 mile. Turn right onto North Street and follow it a short distance to the Stony Brook Nature Center parking lot on the right. Pamphlets (25¢ each) for the self-guiding trail are sold in the nature center building at the corner of the parking lot.

Walk around behind the building to begin the hike. Before turning left at the start of the trail, gaze toward the pond below to the right. Canada geese and a variety of ducks can be seen grazing on the shore or tipping up to reach pond vegetation below the water. In late spring,

Canada Geese

goslings accompany the parent geese. Their fluffy yellow appearance quickly changes to grayish brown as they begin to assume their characteristic coloring patterns. The youngsters move about like ungainly teenagers, preferring to eat lying down. Proceed cautiously if you see the parents' long, black necks bolt upright in alarm.

Follow the path between high stone walls bounding fields. From April 15 to July 15 these fields are reserved solely for breeding purposes and are off-limits to all humans. Continue straight ahead (past the rope-connected fenceposts leading right) to the short, wooden bridge crossing the overflow of water from Teal Marsh to Kingfisher Pond. Look left to the domed muskrat lodges and raised wood duck boxes. Wood ducks are the only ducks that have a long, slicked-back crest. The multi-colored drake is the most striking duck of this area.

The path covered with wood chips reaches a fork and bears left onto a boardwalk. Move

stealthily as you walk across the marsh. By carefully scanning the area ahead, you'll feel the excitement of suddenly locating a motionless form blending with its surroundings. Green frogs sit almost submerged at your feet. Painted turtles lie with necks outstretched and snap at insects flying past.

At the boardwalk's end, take either fork of the short loop trail to the platform overlooking the water. This peaceful spot invites you to linger among the sights and sounds of Kingfisher Pond.

Cross back over the boardwalk and turn left at the trail junction. The jumble of boulders ahead offers another restful vantage point overlooking the pond.

Retrace your steps to the trail, go left, and follow its tree-lined route to a second footbridge. Kingfisher Pond remains to your left while Stony Brook Pond is on the right.

The path re-enters the pine woods beyond the bridge and

Stony Brook Nature Center

edges along beside the water. It dips down into a moist forest before crossing the bridge over Stony Brook. To the left, a manmade stone canal guides the flow of wa-ter from the dam. Several mills operated here in centur-ies past. Portions of their stone foundations still remain beside the path as it swings right and climbs above a stepped waterfall.

The path winds through an open meadow and returns to the rear of the nature center.

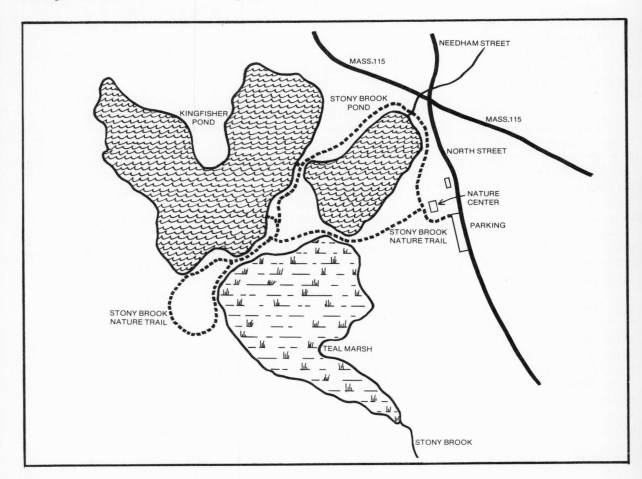

Stony Brook Nature Center

13. Ravenswood Park

Class: II
Distance (round trip): 2.75 miles
Hiking time: 1½ hours

In 1889 the 300 acres of wooded land, rocky knolls, and swamp making up Ravenswood Park were given by Samuel E. Sawyer "for the benefit of all who want to walk and enjoy the woods." His original hopes for the land have been carried forth for nearly a century. Today, anyone can roam the more than five miles of trails and interconnecting paths (where motor vehicles are prohibited) free of charge. The park is open from sunrise to sunset.

Take exit 16 (to Manchester and Magnolia) off Mass 128 and turn north onto Mass 127. Follow this road approximately 6 miles to the Ravenswood Chapel in Magnolia, on the left. Pull into the parking area beside the chapel. The park entrance is at the far end of the lot.

Go straight on Valley Road. This wide, stone-edged, dirt lane travels through woods filled with white birches and eastern hemlocks. Turn onto the second path leading right (Otter Pond Path) just beyond a towering hemlock at the trail's edge. This narrow

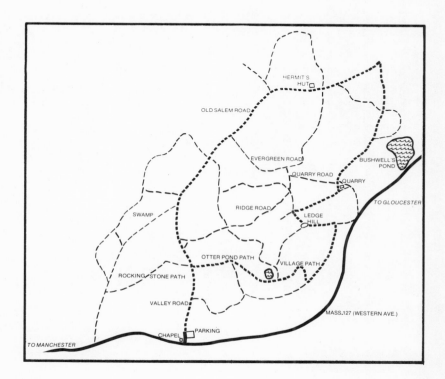

path travels through thin woods filled with large glacial boulders. Sheep laurel and mountain laurel brighten the way. Carefully placed stones edge the trail. Larger, moss-covered rocks signal your approach to a small pond.

Rocks become more prominent as you wind through an area resembling a cemetery. A huge glacial boulder rises at the

trail junction ahead. Swing right onto the Village Path. This narrow, grassy path passes through woods filled with stones and glacial boulders. After crossing the second of two old stone walls, turn left onto the wider trail.

Pine needles cover the way, and pink lady's slippers—two-leaved and puffy-petaled—sprout in the woods. More old stone

Ravenswood Park

walls abut the path as it heads toward a fork just below a rocky knoll. Go left and climb easily up the rock-filled trail to Ledge Hill.

Notice the bumpy, olive-green lichen covering the rocks. Appropriately named "toad skin lichen" its flat disks are covered with blisters and pits, looking indeed like a toad's back. Lichens usually grow where other plants do not furnish competition. They are slow-growing, sun-loving, long-lived plants which flourish wherever the air is clean.

Cresting the hill, the trail slides between two large boulders with white streaks on them. Two paths lead straight and diagonally left here. Go straight. Small rocks, hordes of blueberries, and other side growth try to conceal the trail at times. Watch for occasional white blazes on rocks along the way.

When you reach a wider dirt path, turn right. This crunchy dirt-and-sand trail becomes

Quarry

less rocky as it winds through thick woods. Suddenly a fork appears and you stare into a water-filled quarry. Ledged on three sides, it slants down toward Quarry Road beyond. Take the left trail to Quarry Road (you might first want to walk right for a better view of the quarry itself) and continue straight across onto Flat Rock Path.

The grassy trail quickly becomes rocky and moss-covered. It dodges several boulders, drops into a damp area, and crosses a brook. Blue flag thrives here. This member of the iris family closely resembles the domesticated variety and grows in marshes, along streams, and in other wet places.

The way suddenly widens beneath mature hemlocks. Younger hemlocks try to smother the path ahead. Bull through them and climb the slight, rocky grade. Slender white birches appear just before a narrow path crosses the trail. Stay straight to the junction with the Old Salem Road.

Turn left onto this wide, flat

road. Stay straight at the junction where Evergreen Road enters from the left. Just beyond, a stone tablet sets to the right of the road. Placed there by the Gloucester Women's Club in 1933, it honors Mason A. Walton, the Hermit of Gloucester (and lover of nature) who lived in a nearby cabin for thirty-three years. Self heal (formerly used to cure sore throats and other minor complaints) grows in front of the marker.

After 2¼ miles the Evergreen Road joins again from the left. Ahead the trail to Magnolia Swamp exits right. (This route will take you alongside swampy woods where the intense silence is broken only occasionally by bird or squirrel sounds. The connecting paths across the swamp become quite soft and muddy in spots. Stay straight on Valley Road for the return trip to your car.)

Ravenswood Park

Crane Reservation.

Crane Reservation is located in Ipswich, a town rich in both ancient and colonial history. Archaeological excavations in 1958 established the existence of a primitive culture nearly 9,000 years old. The town's first white settlers were a spunky lot who smuggled small parts of knitting machines across the Atlantic in butter churns. This subterfuge, in defiance of England's export laws, enabled them to set up their own knitting mills. The Ipswich Rebellion Tablet marks the spot of another stand for independence and liberty. Here in 1687, townspeople led by John Wise protested the tyrannical rule of Royal Governor Sir Edmund Andros.

About 1900 Ipswich became a popular summer resort. Richard T. Crane, Jr., acquired all of Castle Hill in 1910. He subsequently purchased Castle Neck and other areas totaling 1,000 acres. After his death in 1945, his wife Florence gave the land and the Crane residence to the Trustees of Reservations. Today the Crane

Crane Reservation Tracks

14. Crane Reservation

Class: I
Distance (round trip): 1 mile
Hiking time: ¾ hour

Reservation includes 1,326 acres of beach, sand dunes, pitch pine forests, red maple swamp, hills, and dales which offer a natural area where wild animals and plants can live peacefully and where man can discover some of this peace.

Turn off Mass 1A at the sign for Crane Beach opposite the Ipswich Green. Drive 4 miles northeast to the Crane Reservation at the end of the road. Stop at the booth and pay the $2 day-parking fee. All proceeds from this collection are "used exclusively for the restoration of [Crane Beach's] natural environment and to meet its annual management expenses."

The Pine Hollow Interpretive Trail helps you come to know the reservation's natural environment. A quality guidebook to this trail may be purchased for 25¢ at the beach office to the left of the parking lot.

The trail begins at the right side of the parking area near the beach. On cooler days, enjoy this trek in your bare feet. (On a scorching summer

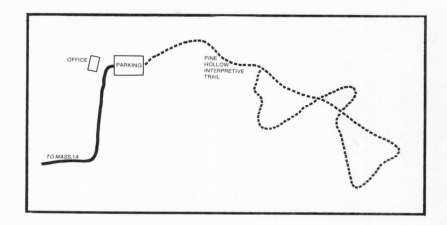

day, however, sand surface temperatures may reach 150 degrees.) Whether barefoot or shod, remember that most of this hike takes you through sand. It is not easy walking!

Arrowed and numbered red and white posts guide you along the way. Station 1 demonstrates some procedures of a sand dune restoration and stabilization program begun in 1969. Sand dunes are extremely vulnerable to wind and water erosion, and abuses by man. Snow fences, split rail barriers, boardwalks, and beach grass (its generic name *Ammophila* means "lover of sand") help halt the destructive movement of the dunes.

Leaving station 1 the trail climbs over a dune straight ahead, just right of some scrubby trees. Note where shore birds have tracked random patterns in the sand.

Approach station 2 and pivot slowly to take in a rather expansive view. Plum Island Sound and Plum Island (beyond) lie to the west (left). The nearest hill to the left (closest to the ocean) is Steep Hill. Castle Hill, the highest point on Castle Neck, rises south of Steep Hill.

After passing station 6, the sandy trail swings down to the right past bayberry, poison ivy, and wooly hudsonia.

Crane Reservation

The path winds away from the beach area and becomes alternately firm over hard sand, and wobbly in softer sand.

During your walk through the dunes, you may see tunneling sand dune spiders. You're more likely to see the burrow openings (approximately ⅜ inches in diameter) than the nocturnal, eight-legged insect.

This unconventional spider does not weave a web; it ambushes or runs down prey.

Beyond station 14 the trail squeezes between bushes and passes over a short, wooden footbridge. Crossing the original path, you enter the shade of a pitch pine forest at station 16. Winter winds, sand, ice, and salt spray prey upon these trees. If they do not grow

quickly, the migrating sand dunes may inundate the forest.

Leave the pitch pine forest and wind your way through the red maple swamp over short boardwalks to the junction with the original trail. Retrace your steps over the dunes to the parking lot.

15. Old Town Hill Reservation

Class: II
Distance (round trip): 1 mile
Hiking time: ¾ hour

Old Town Hill in Newbury served as a mariners' landmark for more than two centuries. Its flat top (168 feet above sea level) once supported a huge elm, visible far out to sea. At the end of the nineteenth century it was open pasture land, but a variety of trees have since taken over certain areas. Its attractive setting encourages both pleasant hiking and scenic viewing.

The Trustees of Reservations administer the 230 acres included in this area. This nonprofit organization was created in 1891 to preserve the state's historical and natural places for public use, and today controls nearly 12,000 acres. The trustees have always sought quality rather than quantity when acquiring and maintaining particularly beautiful and refreshing areas with wide public appeal.

Driving north on Mass 1A in Newbury, cross the Parker River and turn left onto Newman Road (the first left beyond river). The entrance to Old Town Hill Reservation appears quickly on the right, across from a high stone wall

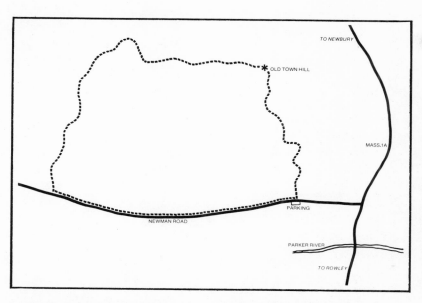

bordering open farmland. Park along the side of the road near the sign.

The trail leads through a small field and over a narrow path paved in woodchips. Climbing moderately, it twists between stands of eastern red cedar.

Pasture roses appear along the trails. Found in upland pastures and dry, rocky ground, this shrub grows to three feet high with pink, aromatic flowers measuring two inches across. The rose can be dis-

tinguished from others by the sharp, straight thorns which grow only where the leaves branch off from the stems.

Common juniper fill the sides of the path, often providing a base for the pasture roses. This gray-green sprawling shrub usually grows on rocky soils.

Twisting moderately upward, the path passes other species of trees which have been allowed to grow in specified areas. Quaking aspen and staghorn sumac temporarily pre-

dominate along the way. Roses continue to intermingle freely with the bristly-looking junipers.

After negotiating several twisting turns, you reach a long bench. Sit for a moment and enjoy the view back to the Parker River and rolling countryside beyond. A bit left, you see marshland meeting ocean, with Castle Neck in the distance.

A short walk brings you to the top of Old Town Hill. More benches set along the left side of the clearing here, but for better views walk along the narrow path to the right. Looking up the coast to the north you'll see Mount Agamenticus in Maine. The Isles of Shoals lie somewhat closer off New Hampshire's coast. To the east and south you can see Plum Island and on down to Cape Ann. The closer view is filled with tidal creeks meandering through uninterrupted marshlands.

The trail continues across the hilltop, just to the right of the

Early Morning Shadows

benches. Travel the dirt and grass path into taller, thicker woods. Bend under the boughs of overhanging apple trees and proceed to a short spur leading right to a large field filled with ox-eye daisies. The view beyond encompasses a traditional New England pastoral scene: thick woods, open meadows, and towns of white clapboard houses.

As you walk along the ridge, views sometimes disappear behind clumps of aspen and sumac. But you'll continue to hear the long, loud, bubbling call of an area resident; the bobolink resides in hay fields and, during fall migrations, near marshes. In the spring, the male is the only North American bird dark below and light above. The females (and males in fall) resemble large sparrows, but have buffy breasts and crown stripes, and narrow, pointed tail feathers.

The path dips, curves right, and begins a downhill route.

Swinging left, it becomes thickly grassed-over before returning to a packed dirt surface. A walk through typical deciduous forests brings you back to Newman Road.

Go left onto the macadam road and begin the walk back to your car.

Old Town Hill Reservation

Phillips Academy Bird Sanctuary

16. Phillips Academy Bird Sanctuary

Class: I
Distance (round trip): 2.25 miles
Hiking time: 1¼ hours

The months of May and early June bring added beauty to this verdant area, for it is then that the azaleas, rhododendron, and laurel burst forth. Wide gravel paths, many softened by fallen hemlock needles, circle and crisscross the sanctuary. Artificial ponds and shaded walkways kindle an atmosphere of secluded tranquility. Birds abound.

At Phillips Academy, located south of Andover center on Mass 28, turn east onto Chapel Avenue at the Andover Inn sign. Drive past the inn to the parking lot beyond George Washington Hall on the right.

Continue straight on Chapel Avenue Extension past the Henry L. Stimson House on the right. Follow the circular road to the metal gates supported by stone pillars which mark the sanctuary's entrance.

Pass through the stone-enclosed door to the left and walk between rows of rhododendron to the sanctuary fence. The gate opens at 7 a.m. and is locked at 6 p.m. No dogs are allowed. Walk up

Mountain Laurel

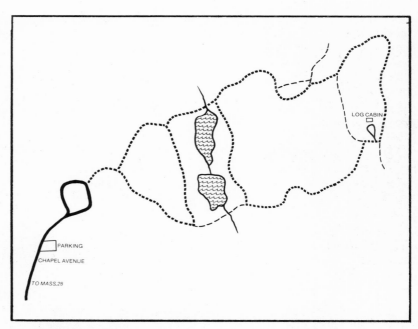

the main path to the bulletin board which displays a map of the sanctuary.

Begin the circuit route by taking the gravel road which forks right from the bulletin board. The ever present great rhododendron continues to line the path.

Taller trees rise above the flowers; many are labeled to help you identify them. Eastern hemlocks droop their branches over the trail as

you approach a path on the left. Turn here and walk over cushiony spills from these majestic hemlocks and eastern white pines.

The quacking of ducks through trees to the right alerts you to the first of two artificial ponds. The long, easy grade bypasses the tip of this pond and passes between dense rows of pink azaleas.

As you reach the next trail junction, walk gradually downhill to the right. A side path leads to the second pond, where ripples on the water suggest animal and insect activity.

Return to the main trail and go right, past the spillway and over the granite bridge. Swing right at the fork atop a gentle rise and travel past rhododendrons growing ten to twelve feet high. At the end of the path turn left.

Common crows are among the noisiest birds in the sanctuary. These scavengers will "caw" repeatedly during your leisurely jaunt. They walk, rather than hop, on the ground and post a sentry when feeding.

The flat path passes rows of multi-hued azaleas and a grove of American larches, also called tamaracks and hackmatacks. These slender, cone-shaped trees are members of the pine family, but shed their needles in the fall. Indians used their rough roots to bind birchbark canoes.

Bear right at the junction by a two-chimneyed, brown structure and wind left around a small log cabin. Follow the

looping path through an open field back into the woods. Finishing its sweeping bend, the trail reaches another junction. Go right here, then straight where another path joins from the right a short distance ahead.

The way dips and curves right. Becoming grassier, it passes through woods filled with ferns. For the first time since

Mallards

starting the walk, flowers do not brighten the way.

Turning right at the rounded fork ahead returns you to your former route past the spillway and pond. Turn right at the crest of the long, moderate grade and wind left, past blazing azaleas which resemble orchid corsages, to the bulletin board where the walk began.

Phillips Academy Bird Sanctuary

17.   Great Meadows National Wildlife Refuge

Class: I
Distance (around marsh): 1.5 miles
Hiking time: ¾ hour

Rustling reeds part as a musk-rat's sleek brown body slides into a quiet pool. Spreading ripples forecast the approach of a slow-paddling mallard along a grass-covered inlet. Looking like a part of the log it reclines on, a painted turtle lies basking in the sunshine. A blue-spotted salamander gropes along the water's muddy bottom near shore, safe for the present from its nocturnal predator, the rac-coon. Out beyond the rim of brush and grass, fast-beating wings slow to a glide as water-fowl skid across open water. The musical symphony of songbirds electrifies the other-wise tranquil scene.

You're standing atop the ob-servation tower at the Great Meadows National Wildlife Refuge in Concord. With each scanning of the marsh, your eyes notice something new.

From this twenty-five-foot high vantage point you can sur-vey your route through the marsh. You'll travel across the long, gravel causeway bisecting the open water ahead, swing right at its end and cir-cle the eastern half of the ref-

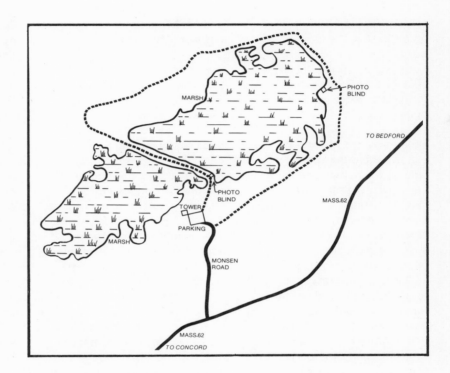

uge. Photo blinds along the trail provide opportunities to observe and photograph ani-mal life at close range. We suggest rising with the sun and hiking through the refuge when its inhabitants are bus-tling about.

The winding Concord River keeps the refuge alive, just as it has done for thousands of years. Spring floods nour-

ish the land and help each new growing season begin. A wide variety of grains, plants, seeds, and roots provide boun-teous meals for native and migrant animals. Over 200 species of birds have been identified within the refuge since its inception in 1944.

From the center of Concord, drive northeast on Bedford Road (Mass 62) for 1¼ miles to Monsen Road. Turn left and follow the signs to Great Meadows Wildlife Refuge. From the right edge of the parking lot, take the Dike Trail past information boards out into the open marsh.

Broad-leaved and narrow-leaved cattails thicken the land on both sides. The slender brown "cat's tail" is actually thousands of tiny female flowers topped by a lighter colored spike containing the male flowers. Cattails play vital roles within the refuge ecosystem. Muskrats eat their roots and stems, and use them for construction materials; nesting birds and ducks seek their protective cover, and the ever-present red-winged blackbirds perch on their slender stems.

A photo blind sets beside the first bend in the trail. Climb up quietly. You should see (among many other things) the common gallinule. This short-necked, long-legged, henlike bird frequents freshwater marshes and lake shores. It is easily identified by the red frontal plate on the head, the yellow-tipped, chickenlike bill,

and horizontal white feather line along the wing.

Walk along the gravel causeway crossing the marsh. Ducks and geese swim among the reeds and grass. In spring and summer you'll see baby birds scurry awkwardly across the path. Like most national wildlife refuges, this one was established primarily to help migratory waterfowl survive.

Vast quantities of duckweed appear along the shore as you turn right at the sign for "restrooms and photo blind." The The green floating specks take nutrients from the water through short, hairlike rootlets. Waterfowl thrive on both these tiny, floating herbs and the numerous insects congregating among them.

Muskrat houses occupy the northern shore. Built of matted vegetation, they consist of marsh grasses and sedges, sometimes heaped to four feet in height. The hollowed-out inside contains a living chamber. When winter ice coats the water's surface, muskrats exit through a lower level opening to forage for food.

Ducks on the wing catch your eye throughout the refuge. A tingle of excitement and awe always stirs within us when we watch them approach and land. Rapid wingbeats slow to a rigid halt; bodies drop quickly; heads rise and tails dip as the graceful birds lose momentum and ready for the landing. With feet outstretched and wings braced, they skid to a splashy stop.

Circle the far end of the marsh to the log cabin and follow the path to the right. Now you are in thick woods and soon reach the second photo blind. The path winds through densely-ferned forests before joining with the entrance road which will return you to your car.

Canada Geese

Great Meadows National Wildlife Refuge

Great Meadows National Wildlife Refuge

In 1845 Henry Thoreau set about constructing his plain dwelling on land owned by his good friend, Ralph Waldo Emerson. During his two-year sojourn at Walden Pond, Thoreau sought the solitude and simplicity he needed for thinking and writing. But he was no hermit, and frequently returned to Concord to fraternize with the group of liberal poets, novelists, essayists, naturalists, and philosophers who congregated there during the mid-nineteenth century.

The overwhelming numbers of visitors who now converge on the area in summer months seriously threaten Walden Pond. Uncaring persons, separated from Thoreau's civilized vision by more than a hundred years of history and light years of understanding, leave bottles, cans, cigarette butts, and other trash in the pond and around its edges. The Society for the Preservation of Walden Pond is working closely with the County Commissioners (who are presently in charge) to protect the area from overuse. An admission charge, and a limit on the people who may enter at one time, will probably be instituted. Such measures may help to restore and protect the natural beauty appreciated there by the man who stepped to the music of a different drum.

From the intersection of Mass

The Pond

Walden Pond

18. Walden Pond

Class: I
Distance (around pond): 1 mile
Hiking time: ½ hour

126 and Mass 2 in Concord, drive .3 miles south on route 126 to a large parking area on the right. Follow a path from the parking lot down a steep embankment to Walden Pond. The spring-fed waters of the pond fill a 100-foot glacial kettle and attract swimmers, fishermen, boaters (canoes and rowboats only), and picnickers.

Turn right following the white-encircled Ts which mark the pond's circuit loop. Stepped railroad ties gird the pond edge and retard erosion. The trail's right side slopes steeply upward. You enjoy continuous open views across the pond to the left.

The trail winds around to the right and crosses a short land bar dividing Walden Pond from a small area of marshy water. Ahead the path winds right and away from the pond, following the white trail markers to the site of Thoreau's cabin. (A model of the cabin has been constructed behind the Thoreau Lyceum, a center for Thoreau history, books, and information on Belknap Street in Concord.) Behind the

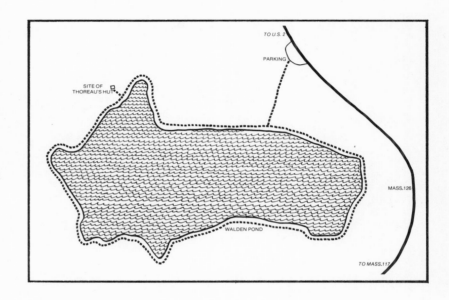

stone marking the original site lies a mound of medium-sized stones. Some people believe adding a rock to the pile brings good fortune; others think taking one away achieves the same end.

Returning to the shore, the path continues curving around the coved edge. Turtles and frogs sit motionless in sun-warmed shallows. They use the heat to accelerate their "cold-blooded" body functions.

A passing train may reveal the presence of the Boston and Maine railroad tracks atop a rise just above the pond. In Thoreau's day, steam-powered trains puffed along the same route.

The path twists by delicately-needled eastern hemlocks and emerges into the opening near the buildings at the swimming area. A short walk beside the beach returns you to your starting point at the foot of the embankment.

Walden Pond

Central Massachusetts

Quabbin Reservoir

Towering walls

Others, familiar with the *Divine Comedy* and of a less geological bent, believe that men guilty of worldly pride deposited the rocks there after carrying them through Dante's imagined purgatory.

A walk through Purgatory Chasm will nurture your urge to explore. First awe, then intrigue, grip the visitor to this natural phenomenon. An immense fissure splits towering walls of solid rock. Jumbled heaps of boulders lay strewn about the valley floor as if tossed there by some careless giant. Caves and depressions beneath and among the rocks invite your inspection.

On Mass 146, drive approximately 7 miles north from its junction with Mass 16 or 6 miles south from the Massachusetts Turnpike (US 90) to the signs for Purgatory Chasm. Follow them west to the Purgatory Chasm State Reservation. This area contains both scenic woodlands featuring odd rock formations and facilities for relaxation within a peaceful setting. Pic-

Local town histories give no clue to the origin of deep, boulder-filled Purgatory Chasm near Whitinsville. Some attribute the phenomenon to earthquakes or glaciers.

Purgatory Chasm

19. Purgatory Chasm

Class: III
Distance (round trip): .75 miles
Hiking time: ½ hour

nic tables, fireplaces, spring water, and swings await your use.

Bypass the first parking area on the right and stop at the next one to the left. A sloping-roof building with stone pillars sets near one end of this lot. The trail through and around Purgatory Chasm begins beside this structure.

Follow the silver paint splotches to the edge of the chasm. Ahead is the first of three craggy ravines which lead you progressively deeper into the bowels of the gorge. Climb slowly over jumbled boulders down into the dank coolness of this sixty-foot wide by eighty-foot deep fissure.

Shadowy chamber openings entice the adventurous of spirit and fit of body to enter. A flashlight will help reveal the mysteries of these darkened passages.

Step down into the chasm's midsection and look directly overhead. Jagged walls support tons of overhanging rock. Trees cling tenaciously to tiny patches of dirt and seem

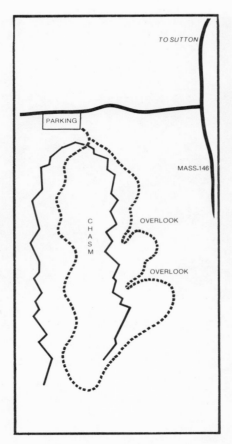

to grow right out of the stone.

A huge eastern hemlock spreads tentacle-like roots across the rocky floor and rises majestically to the ravine's rim. Although hemlocks usually grow sixty to seventy-five feet high

and three feet in diameter, this monster has soared past normal dimensions in this verdant setting.

Surroundings shrink away as you make your way to the third portion of the chasm. The biggest cave of all awaits your exploration here. A silver arrow to the right points the way.

Follow the trail around to the left and begin the return route along the fissure's eastern rim. Climb over and around heaps of large rocks. After swinging widely right to circle a ledged outcropping, the trail veers left to an overlook. Step carefully over a foot-wide, smooth-sided crevice and walk toward the canyon's edge. Tree roots offer firm footing, but handholds are scarce. Look—but don't lean—into the gorge.

A second overlook appears near the halfway point of the return trip.

The fragile beauty of rising hemlocks contrasts sharply with the harsh bareness of intermittent boulders as you follow the well-marked trail back to your car.

Purgatory Chasm

Wachusett Meadows Wildlife Sanctuary

20. Wachusett Meadows Wildlife Sanctuary

Class: I
Distance (round trip): 2.5 miles
Hiking time: 1¼ hours

The Wachusett Meadows Wildlife Sanctuary offers an array of plant and animal habitats. This 2½-mile combination of trails takes you to upland pastures, meadows, ponds, thickets, woodlands, and a maple swamp. Nearly one hundred species of birds and a wide assortment of animals are seen here each year.

From the intersection of Mass 31 and Mass 62 in Princeton, go west .6 miles on route 62 to Goodnow Road. Turn right and follow this road approximately 1 mile to the sanctuary parking lot on the left. A number of trails radiate from this point.

Take the grassy path (Swamp Nature Trail) south from the parking lot across the high-grassed, open field. At the far end, the trail enters a maple swamp and proceeds atop an attractive, winding boardwalk. The numbered stations through here correspond to the sanctuary's self-guiding nature trail pamphlet.

Like feathery, green fans, ferns

Swamp Nature Trail

ruffle in the slightest breeze. Listen for the flutelike, descending notes of the veery. Compared to the wood thrush and the hermit thrush, the veery's breast is more buff colored and less distinctly spotted. Of the three species, you're most likely to see the veery in the red maple swamp.

A short boardwalk spur leads left to a wooden observation platform. Continue right on the main boardwalk.

You'll see examples of the unique pitcher plant to the right of this fork. It derives its name from the four- to twelve-inch cylindrical leaves. They can catch water, but are famous for capturing and digesting insects. The trapped prey may also be used as food for the larvae of the flies responsible for cross-pollinating the plant. A single, long-stalked, rose-purple flower has five spreading, greenish sepals and five inward-curving, purple petals enclosing the yellow center.

Royal fern grows abundantly in this swamp area. Its large leaves may grow to six feet

in height.

Leaving the swamp, hike over a softer, needle-covered path. Climb an easy grade to the left and swing right along a stone wall edging an open field. At the junction ahead, go left onto the Crocker Trail.

Walk through a field on a grassy dirt road. If you look along the muddy ruts of the trail, you may see evidence of passing raccoons and foxes (and saddle horses!).

At Fire Pond, take some time to observe the water creatures. Late in the spring or early in the summer the sun-warmed shallows attract salamanders and tadpoles.

The trail, still an overgrown road, soon enters another old pasture. Ahead to the left is the small hut known as Mountain View House. This structure's cross studs are popular places for the eastern phoebe's mud and moss nest. Originally, phoebes nested on rock shelves or in ravine cavities, but they now favor civilization's rafters, window sills, and shutter tops.

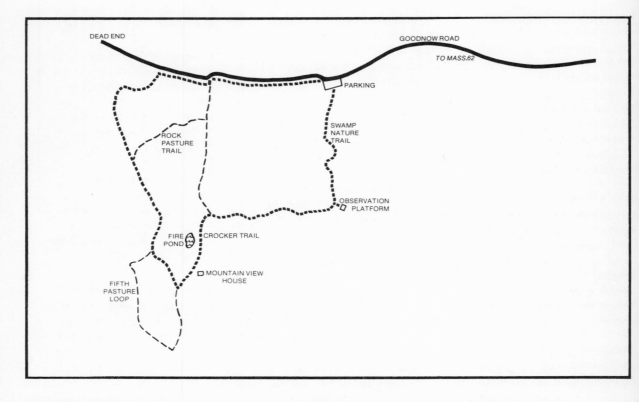

Hike to the right of the Mountain View House following the path across the field. Just after leaving the field, bear right at a grassy fork. (A left would take you to the Fifth Pasture Loop, closed off seasonally to allow goshawks to breed.)

Silver disks blaze the way. As you follow the narrow, grassy path past apple trees, you may be startled by fleeing deer.

Pass through another stone wall and bear left into the twilight of thick grove of eastern hemlocks. Beyond, a stand of smooth, grey American beeches edges the trail. A brown-leaf carpet alternates with short, muddy sections as you continue to meander through the hardwood forest.

Meeting a stone wall, the trail swings right to parallel it. The Crocker Trail ends at a broad, grassy fire lane. Turn left onto this path, then right onto the dirt road beyond. Follow the road, past another fire lane and a house on the right, to the sanctuary parking lot.

Wachusett Meadows Wildlife Sanctuary

21.   Wachusett Mountain

Class: III
Elevation: 2,006 feet
Vertical rise: 796 feet
Distance (round trip): 3.2 miles
Hiking time: 1¾ hours

Located in the low altitudes of central Massachusetts, Wachusett Mountain boasts the most expansive summit view east of the Connecticut River and south of New Hampshire. It is the major attraction of the Wachusett Mountain State Reservation, a tract of over 2,100 acres in the towns of Princeton and Westminster. The following trails challenge your muscles and stamina; your reward is the 360-degree panorama from atop the 2,006-foot mountain.

To reach the start of this hike, go 1.3 miles north from Princeton center on Mountain Road and turn left at the fork onto Westminster Road. Drive .8 miles and park in the area just in front of gated Administration Road.

Walk around the gate and up to the old moss-veined, macadam road, past a gravel road leading right. The rounded, rectangular holes in dead trees along the way attest the presence of the pileated woodpecker. These striking birds bore large holes in pursuit of carpenter ants, their favorite food. Silent (except in the spring

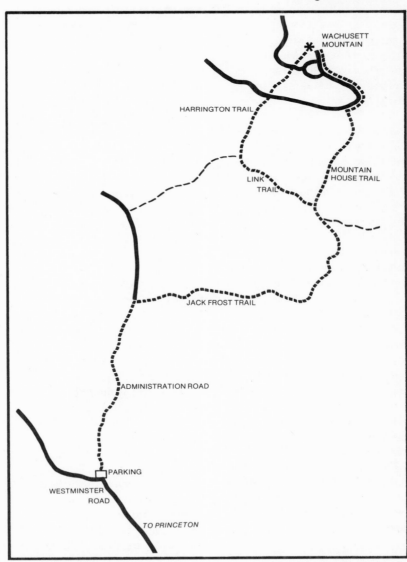

Wachusett Mountain

when they call and drum) and wary, these seventeen-inch, red-crested, black and white wood-peckers are seldom seen. Males have additional red streaks along the sides of the throat.

Stay on Administration Road for .3 miles, until you reach the brown and white sign point-ing right for the Jack Frost Trail. Turn here and follow the grassy road narrowed by mountain laurel.

Take the right fork ahead, following the Jack Frost Trail's light blue blazes. You quick-ly ford two small streams and pass beneath power lines. Enter the hushed light and cushioned sounds of the hem-lock forest. Ascend the steep-ledged and rooted trail to the top of a 690-foot hill (no views).

From this summit, the trail bears more northerly toward Wachusett Mountain. Flatter walking along the hill's ridge offers a respite from the rigors of the recent climb. Butter-flies dance on wildflower blos-soms beside the path.

After a gentle descent through a smaller grove of hemlocks and yet another leg-stretching climb, the Jack Frost Trail intersects with the Mountain House Trail after 1¼ miles of hiking. Swing left onto the Mountain House Trail, pass-ing the eastern end of the yellow-blazed Link Trail on the left.

Climb straight over the rocky path through many young beeches. Soon you'll emerge onto the tarred Summit Road. Turn right, then sharply left, following signs to the top.

The upper section of the Har-rington Trail makes up the first leg of the short loop back to the Jack Frost Trail. This rapid, rugged descent from the summit demands a goodly amount of agility and strength. (If any member of your group is physically out of shape, retrace your route back down the Mountain House Trail to the Jack Frost Trail).

Leave the summit area by walk-ing down the narrow path be-tween the stone wall and the corner of the fire tower enclo-sure. Cross the road below and continue across a small picnic area to the brown and white sign for the Harrington Trail.

This first short descent ends quickly at the Summit Road. The rigorous route resumes its steep pitch beyond the road. Roots and rounded depressions in the ledges offer good hand and footholds. Occasional white blazes and cairns guide you down this rocky maze. At the bottom of an especially precipitous drop over a mossy sheet of ledge, the trail swings abruptly left and slabs the slope for 100 feet before junctioning with the Link Trail.

Go left onto the yellow-blazed Link Trail and climb easily over the rocky path. Pass diagonally to the left, beneath a power line. You will quickly meet the Mountain House Trail. Turn right onto this trail and them immediately right again onto the Jack Frost Trail. From here, re-trace your original route back to the parking area.

Climbing the Jack Frost Trail

Crow Hill

22. Crow Hill

Class: III
Elevation: 1,220 feet
Vertical rise: 620 feet
Distance (round trip): 2.75 miles
Hiking time: 1½ hours

Towering, sheer ledges rise eighty feet above the trail from Redemption Rock to Crow Hill near its terminus. These are the cliffs that stir the blood of rock climbers. For hikers interested in less arduous pursuits, these ledges stand as monuments of nature's architectural prowess. Superb wilderness views await all who climb to the uppermost ledges. Late May and June bring the added bonus of flowering mountain laurel to the roller coaster trail.

From the northern junction of Mass 140 and Mass 31 in Princeton, drive .8 miles north on route 140 to the Trustees of Reservations sign for Redemption Rock. Turn into the small parking area.

The trail to Crow Hill begins on the east side of route 140, next to the first telephone pole north of the house across from the parking area. White arrows and blazes point the way up over a short, steep ledge. You'll use hands as well as feet to surmount this initial obstacle.

View from Crow Hill

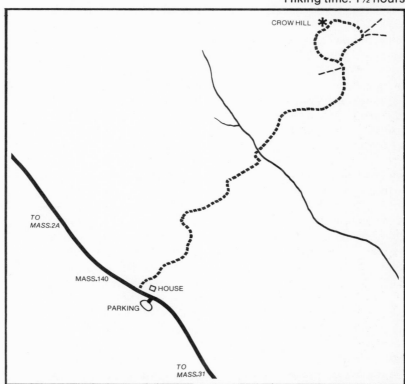

Climbing steeply through thick clumps of mountain laurel, the path passes up over two huge hunks of ledge. Atop the second, look back for an unobstructed view of Wachusett Mountain.

Swinging left off the ledge, the path passes through trail-edging huckleberry bushes. This shrub, whose tangy black berries provide a tasty midsummer snack, usually grows in dry, rocky, or sandy soil.

The trail descends gently through woodlands filled with laurel. Leveling out, it turns sharply left at a white blaze

Crow Hill

and climbs up over more ledge. Cresting this rocky hilltop, the way turns left and levels out again.

You step through two sections of a stone wall before descending moderately to a damp, rocky area. Go right at the fork ahead.

Different kinds of ferns fill the trail sides. Lady fern, growing twelve to thirty-six inches high, is prominent. Christmas tree-shaped leaflets decorate the delicate looking fronds growing individually from the plant's base.

Leveling out, the path crosses two small brooks, bears left at a stone wall, and crosses a faster stream after ¾ of a mile. The water spreads out as it slides down over wide, flat ledge. Remove your boots and cool hot feet here.

Inspect muddy areas in and along the trail for animal tracks. One species to watch for in this area is the red fox. Its four-toed prints will show in two sizes. The sprawling front foot will be wider than the more pointed hind foot.

Rocks fill the trail and signal the start of another climb. The narrow path winds through laurel to a flat, ledged area. Pine needles blanket the dirt as the path descends to pick its way along the base of the mammoth ledges.

Step up onto the overhang which forms a partial cave. It is easy to envision prehistoric man living in such a setting. Sheltered from the elements on three sides and from animals below, a family could have huddled against the rock walls for warmth. Furs might have carpeted the flat floor and the large boulder to the right would have served as both skinning table and tool-making bench. A short, bearded, sturdy-legged fellow clad in a loin cloth walking up the path would complete the scene.

Continue following the white blazes as they lead right, around the bottom of the walls. At a narrow fork, marked by a tree in the center, bear left. Climb the conveniently placed stone steps to the path leading up and around the mountain top.

Reaching the intersection where a medium-sized boulder sits in the middle of the trail, turn sharply left. Pass two overlooks ahead. From east to southwest, you scan a wilderness setting almost devoid of humanity (sharp eyes may spot two or three manmade structures within the miles of forests). Crow Hills Pond extends its fingers to the southeast. Paradise Pond snuggles between green forests straight ahead (south). Swinging southwest, Wachusett Mountain looms above everything in sight. On a clear day you can see Boston's Prudential Building.

Follow the white arrow around the edge. Climb down the steep path and bear right at the white blaze onto your original route. Bear left at the narrow fork just ahead and retrace your previous steps.

Crow Hill

23. Cook's Canyon Wildlife Sanctuary

Class: II
Distance (round trip): 1.5 miles
Hiking time: 1 hour

Your visit to Cook's Canyon Wildlife Sanctuary, in the town of Barre, will include a varied menu of forest, stream, pond, waterfall, and gorge, plus abundant plant and animal life. The forty-acre sanctuary offers a setting conducive to both relaxed recreational outings and study of the natural environment. In winter, the network of trails is available for either snowshoeing or crosscountry skiing.

Drive .3 miles south from Barre Common on South Street to the sanctuary border and turn left into the parking area. Admission fees are charged to those who are not members of the Massachusetts Audubon Society: 50¢ per pedestrian; 50¢ per bicycle or motorcycle; $1 per four-wheel vehicle; $10 per bus. The park closes at dusk.

The boundary trail begins on the road beside the information board. Follow it around the flagpole to the right. The lane passes between several buildings set within heavy conifer forests. Turn left beyond the gaily painted totem pole.

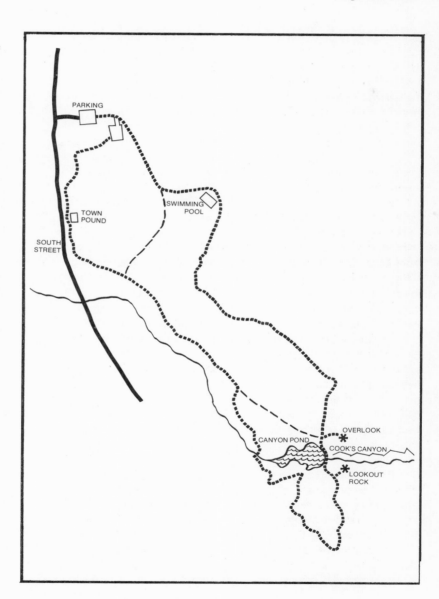

Cook's Canyon Wildlife Sanctuary

Columns of red pines surround you as you head toward the swimming pool. Swing right around the pool building onto the narrow path leading to the end of the fence. Bear right here and pick up the double yellow dots marking the trail.

Continuing stands of red pine stretch high above the stone wall to your left. Watch this rocky old marker for the frantic movements of chipmunks.

After passing the ten platforms head left at the end of the stone wall. The branches of Pacific red elder lean out over the trail as you brush between them. Common in the Pacific Northwest, this shrub grows to a height of twenty-five feet. Elongated clusters of small, white flowers, succeeded by clumps of small red berries, sprout from between the leaves.

The trail travels gradually downhill before crossing damp areas atop wide planks. Pines give way to shady maples as the way edges close to another stone wall. The yellow dots wind left of a large birch and approach a double stone wall. Early farmers toiled to clear stones from their fields. They sometimes built two closely parallel stone walls and filled the opening between with still more stones.

More than one hundred species of birds have been identified within the sanctuary in one year. Listen for the *very very very pleased t' meet cha* call of the chestnut-sided warbler. Both male and female wear a yellowish crown and chestnut side markings in the spring. You'll find them in deciduous brush.

Go right to the wide path ahead and follow it to a clearing. Climb the slight rise onto ledges to the left for a view out across the Ware River Valley. Directly below, water courses through Cook's Canyon. Unfortunately, much of the view of the canyon's nearly two-hundred-foot drop lies blocked behind young tree growth.

Return to the canyon and head left between the two yellow-dotted boulders. The path drops quickly to muddy Canyon Pond. A large stone dam rims the eastern shore and regulates the flow of water into the canyon. Spring melting and rain create a cascading waterfall over this barrier.

Cross the plywood walkway at the lip of the dam. Turn left at the fork ahead and climb up the rocky grade to Lookout Rock. The view from here does not justify the rock's name; young trees cloak the canyon walls.

The trail winds pleasantly through hemlock forests and loops back to Canyon Pond. Wild lily of the valley carpets the forest floor beneath mature trees.

Turn left onto the trail at the pond's edge. This route will take you rock-hopping across the stream feeding into Canyon Pond. Swing left at the fork beyond and climb easily up to a gravel wood road. Go left again.

Automobile sounds signal the trail's approaching end. Nearing the point where South Street crosses the stream, bear left onto the (yellow-dotted) narrower path. This route takes you

Cook's Canyon Wildlife Sanctuary

to the Town Pound. In earlier days, when inquisitive animals ventured into forbidden territory, they were rounded up and herded into this large stone corral until their owners paid a fine.

The narrow path passes through more red pine before ending at a small parking area just around the corner from your car.

Red pine forest

Cook's Canyon Wildlife Sanctuary

Harvard Forest

24. Harvard Forest

Class: I
Distance (round trip): 1.5 miles
Hiking time: 1 hour

The Fisher Museum will highlight your visit to Harvard Forest. Its colorful dioramas depict the history and management of Petersham's forests. These three-dimensional miniature models intricately and realistically detail the land's past and present uses.

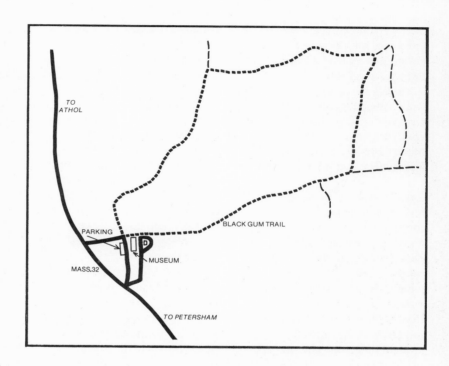

When Petersham's early settlers began clearing the land in 1740, they chose the prime hardwood trees for rough hewing into beams for house framing or for milling into boards and planks. Part of the clearing process involved the burning of wood for which there was no immediate use. Surrounded by bounteous forests, early settlers perceived no need for conservation measures.

Such use of the forests eventually led to a scarcity of wood for construction, fuel, furniture, tools, and industry. The loss of this natural resource was partly responsible for the westward migration of the nineteenth century. The inability of New England farmers to compete with the harvests of the west's rich farmlands

Black Gum Trail

provided additional impetus for the exodus from the farms.

Natural reclamation transformed the abandoned pastures and cropland to forested areas once again. Pine found the idle fields much to its liking. Oak, ash, cherry, and maple subsequently established themselves on the once-cleared acres.

Drive to the headquarters of the

Harvard Forest on the east side of Mass 32, 3 miles north of Petersham center. Park on the road in front of the office and museum. You may wish to explore the exhibits in the Fisher Museum before commencing your hike. Guide maps for the numbered stations along the Black Gum Trail are available here.

Walk left in front of the museum, (away from the office)

Harvard Forest

then turn quickly right onto
the gravel road beside it.
Follow this road past a low,
brick building on the right
to the dirt road entering the
woods ahead. Yellow and red
streamers and arrows mark
your way along this section
of the combined Black Gum
and Natural History trails.

Stop to read the identification plaques along the way.
Stone walls, grape vines,
and an apple tree give evidence of John and Molly San-
derson's subsistence farm
located here 100 years ago.
Just before post #1, the Natural History Trail follows a
red arrow to the right. Go
straight here, following the
yellow arrows and streamers
of the Black Gum Trail.

Red pine predominates, its
branches flaring up and sometimes interlocking above the
trail. Scaly, mature bark
shingles the trunks.

Yellow arrows and/or streamers continue to guide your
way. Partridge berry fre-
quents the trail sides. Pink
or white, paired flowers bloom
at the ends of the creeping

branches. Glossy, evergreen
leaves are arranged in twos
along the stems. A single
red berry forms from the
bottom of each flower.

At station 12, a short side
trail leads to the Black Gum
Swamp. Walk in for a chance
to see the black tupelo, a type
of black gum tree rare in this
region. Oval, dark blue fruit
grow from the bases of the
paired, green flowers. Note
the rectangular plates of its
grey-brown bark.

The hike's final ½ mile travels over graveled access
roads through heavy woods. The
white-throated sparrow is one
of the variety of birds you'll
hear through this area. Listen for its *old sam peabody
peabody peabody* whistled
song. This sparrow abounds
in thick brush and under-
growth.

The circuitous Black Gum
Trail turns left at an intersection and returns you to
your car.

Harvard Forest

25. Quabbin Hill

Class: III
Elevation: 1,030 feet
Vertical rise: 630 feet
Distance (around circuit): 2.75 miles
Hiking time: 1½ hours

Quabbin Reservoir represents exemplary cooperation between the Metropolitan District Commission, other state agencies, and the public. This multiple-purpose facility boasts an immaculate reservoir system which insures maximum use of land and water for taxpayers. The Metropolitan District Commission stresses cleanliness and strictly enforces safety rules.

Quabbin Reservoir is man-made. And that means things were not always as serene as you'll find them now. Unchecked growth and the pollution of its local waters placed the city of Boston in a desperate position during the late 1800s. Thirty-two years after legislators declared the need for a watershed reservoir complex in the Swift River Valley, work began on Quabbin Reservoir. In the meantime, 2,500 people were evacuated from four towns, and six other towns suffered boundary relocations. Seventy-five hundred graves, many marked by curious, old tombstones, were moved to the M. D.C.'s perpetual-care Quabbin Park Cemetery in the town of Ware.

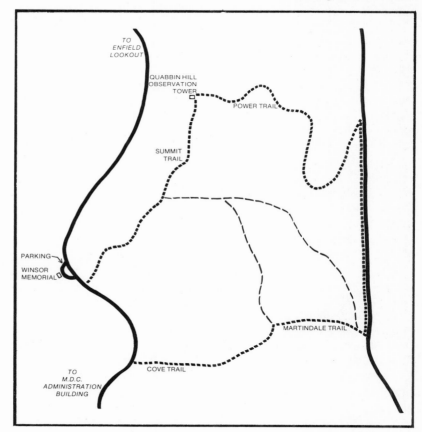

Quabbin, one of the largest reservoirs in the world built specifically for domestic water supply, was completed in 1939. Its name derives from an old Nipmuck Indian chief and means, appropriately, *place of many waters*. The shoreline stretches for 118 miles, not including the perimeters of some sixty rocky and mountainous islands. (The view from Enfield Look Out reminds many of New York State's Thousand Islands.)

Today you can spend leisurely hours relaxing in the miles of wilderness within the Quabbin Reservation. The waters boil with trout, salmon, bass, and perch. Bald eagles soar majestically overhead. Beaver slap the waters of countless brooks and ponds with their tails. White-tailed deer browse the greenery and sometimes stand quizzically transfixed along roadsides. Picnic sites and a network of hiking trails offer opportunities for peaceful enjoyment of this unique area.

On Mass 9, 3 miles east of its junction with US 202 near Belchertown, turn north at the Windsor Dam-Quabbin Reservoir sign. Drive past the M.D.C. Administration Building and across Windsor Dam. Take the first left up the hill at the sign for Quabbin Summit Tower and Drive to the Windsor Memorial. Park here.

The combination of trails selected for this circuit tour of Quabbin Hill is only one of several possible arrangements you might try. To start, walk downhill about ¼ mile to the sign for the Cove Trail. Follow the yellow blazes (left) between rows of stately red pines. The wide trail suddenly narrows and crosses a brook before weaving through continuing stands of red pine.

The path rock-hops across a stream and swings left up onto open ledge above a small pond. Continue along the ledge and down to the right to a trail intersection. The Cove Trail goes straight across here, but take a few extra moments to go left, down to the shore. If the time is right— preferably early morning or late afternoon—you might see the inhabitants of the beaver lodges.

Ripples veer out behind the water-slicked head as a beaver ruffles the pond's stillness. Pushing with webbed hind feet and steering with broad tail, it glides effortlessly around the pond. Following a sudden slap of its tail, the animal dives beneath a shower of water. When leisurely feeding on bottom growth, however, a beaver can disappear with hardly a ripple. Once under water, a specialized respiratory and cardiovascular system enables beavers to remain submerged for 15 minutes, or swim for ½ mile.

Return to the trail junction and swing left onto the narrow path. It climbs gradually through pines and ferns before reaching the junction with the Martindale Trail just beyond the ½ mile point. Go straight (signs point straight and left) onto the Martindale Trail. This grassy road leads down through a meadow to a dirt road.

Go left on the wide, flat road. Ferns proliferate along the edges of thick forests. Watch for the sensitive fern through here. Unlike the feathery look of other ferns, its leaflets are coarse and knifelike with rippled edges.

After approximately 1¼ miles of hiking, turn left onto the signed Power Trail. This cushiony path slabs the hillside, switches back right, and climbs moderately. After you crest a hill, stones fill the path. A final steep climb brings you to a fork. Follow the yellow blazes right, out to the tarred road.

Quabbin Hill

Walk across the open area toward the restrooms. Bear right between two stone pillars and proceed up to the observation tower.

Coin-operated (10¢) binoculars bring closer the expansive views stretching from west to southwest. Mount Tom in Holyoke lies due west. Looking out across the reservoir you see Mount Lincoln to the northwest and Shutesbury Village to the north-northwest. Mount Monadnock in New Hampshire lies just east of north. Petersham village sets a bit east, with Wachusett Mountain in Princeton to the northeast. Ragged Hill in West Brookfield is just south of east and the radio tower for station WARE is to the southeast. A climb up the eighty-one steps to the observation tower will produce an even wider view.

Although you may see bald eagles elsewhere within the reservation, it seems appropriate to watch for them from this highest vantage point. Heart-pounding excitement accompanies the sighting of these striking, powerful birds. John McQuaid of the M.D.C.

Beaver

police has spotted as many as eight of these majestic eagles feeding on the same deer carcass.

For the return trip via the Summit Trail, follow the well beaten path through the blueberry field to the right of the restrooms. At its far end turn right to follow yellow blazes at a fork. The dirt trail leads gradually downhill to the junction with the Martindale Trail.

Continue straight, following the sign for Windsor Dam.

The path approaches a rocky outcropping and swings sharply right. The pitch steepens as you wind downward. Glimpses of the macadam road show through the trees as you turn left and slip below overhanging ledge. Drop down to the right and out to the road near your car.

Quabbin Hill

This Massachusetts Audubon Society educational center offers a stimulating combination of informative exhibits and natural attractions. A polished, yet relaxed, atmosphere sharpens your senses to the learning experiences awaiting you. A variety of visual, tactile, and auditory aids, many three-dimensional, make flora and fauna facts come alive. Both living and stuffed animals invite closer inspection than is normally possible in the wilds. Well-maintained trails ramble through 84 acres of forests and fields reserved exclusively for foot travel. Lots and railings edge the trails wherever the possibility of getting too close to safety hazards exists.

In keeping with the santuary's progressive outlook and concern about environmental conservation, plans call for an eventual underground nature center. Included in this subterranean structure will be a 200-seat auditorium, exhibit hall, and story-telling room. Trails and trees will exist naturally above the hidden building.

From Hampden center, proceed east on Main Street for 1 mile to the sanctuary parking area. The parking fees for those not members of the Massachusetts Audubon Society are: 50¢ per pedestrian and bicycle; $2 per car; and $10 per bus.

Laughing Brook Education Center and Wildlife Sanctuary

26. Laughing Brook Education Center and Wildlife Sanctuary

Class: II
Distance (round trip): 2.1 miles
Hiking time: 1¼ hours

Basking Turtle

Begin walking the Green Forest Trail between the Animal Exhibit Center and the Thornton Burgess home. White metal markers adorned with tiny, painted evergreen trees sign the way. Climb up the stone steps and short, steep hill to the top of the twisted, gravel ridge (geologists call this formation an esker and suspect they were formed by streams running under Ice Age glaciers). At the trail junction ahead, go left onto the Striped Chipmunk Trail.

Yellow metal markers guide you along this flat, comfortable path through hardwood forests. Step over the occasional rocks left in the trail to retain the natural flavor.

Swinging left to parallel a stone wall, the way crosses a muddy section before dropping down into a moist, fern-filled glen. Rocks become more prevalent, giving the path the appearance of an old, dried-up stream bed.

A ledged outcropping rises from the hillside to the left as pine needles begin to cloak the trail. Enjoy the spacious feeling; the wide, well-cleared path creates an openness not found along narrower footpaths.

Reaching the junction with the Green Forest Trail, go right toward the split boulder. Branch left at a fork and inspect this glacial oddity more closely. It appears as if someone took a huge knife and sliced a long, narrow cut down through the boulder. A nearby sign explains how this natural phenomenon actually happened.

Continue around the split boulder loop, turn right onto the Green Forest Trail, and return to the intersection with the Striped Chipmunk Trail. Go straight here.

Wild lily of the valley spreads its shiny, heart-shape-based leaves across the forest floor. Birds sing and chipmunks squeak as you stroll along the flat trail. Look in damp spots for the tracks of animals occasionally seen in this area: deer, raccoon, fox, skunk, opossum, woodchuck, and weasel.

Turning sharply right at a stone wall, the way winds down through thick stands of young white pine and beneath delicate hemlock boughs. Before turning right at the next trail junction you'll hear Laughing Brook. Its waters will accompany you all the way to the Sammy Jay Trail. Highlighted by sparkling sun, the water slides over smooth stretches and ripples around rocks and trees beside the path.

Turn right onto the grassy Sammy Jay Trail and follow the pale blue blazes along stone walls, uphill to the right, and down to the footbridge near Smiling Pond. Turn left at the sign for the nature center and loop your way over bridges and around Smiling Pond. Migratory ducks and geese drop down to enjoy this appealing haven. Even in mid-summer you may see waterfowl around the center island.

Go right onto the Green Forest Trail. Cross one last bridge and follow the wide gravel road down to a large parking area. Turn right

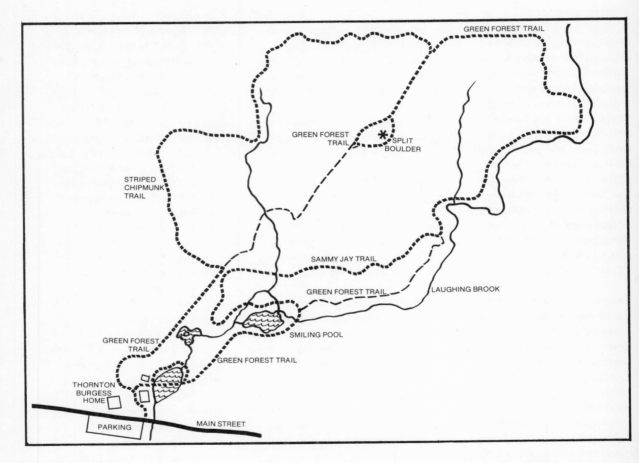

through the trees just before reaching Main Street and walk into the outdoor animal exhibit area. A path circulates between enclosures housing native animals in natural settings. You can view at close range bobcats, raccoons, pocupines, foxes, skunks, and many more. Signs describe the animals' food, breeding, habitat, enemies, and life span. Most of the animals were brought to the sanctuary because they were invalids, orphans, or dependent upon humans.

The path leads over a bridge, between the buildings, and back to the parking lot.

Laughing Brook Education Center and Wildlife Sanctuary

27. The Crooked Little Path (braille trail)

Class: I
Distance (around loop): .3 miles
Hiking time: ½ hour

The information plaques along this "touch and see" trail in the Laughing Brook Education Center employ both braille and large type. The Massachusetts Federation of Women's Clubs sponsored this trail especially for persons who are blind or have impaired vision. But everyone can enjoy and benefit from the many suggestions about exploring nature with all his senses. Those of you who can see might want to close your eyes as you travel the Crooked Little Path. It can also be an exciting hike for children.

In 1968 the Massachusetts Audubon Society began the center and wildlife sanctuary on land formerly owned by Thornton Burgess, a famed writer of children's literature. Burgess had bought the 1742 house and surrounding land in 1929. In the studio near the house, he authored some of the seventy books and 15,000 bedtime stories he wrote over the course of his ninety-one years.

The sanctuary's trails and the animals on exhibition all bear names culled from the pages of Mr. Burgess' works. Along the Crooked Little Path you'll meet Happy Jack (the grey squirrel) and Lightfoot the Deer. You may casually bump into Sammy Jay, Bobby Coon, or Blacky the Crow.

For directions to the Laughing Brook Education Center and Wildlife Sanctuary see Hike 26. Walk across the parking lot to the right of the bulletin board where a sign points right for the start of the trail. Paralleling Laughing Brook and the Scantic River, this gradual path remains easily walkable throughout and allows you to concentrate entirely upon your sensory experiences.

Near one of the first information stops you'll read about the American elm. At another station you learn about the red maple. Its proximity to swampy areas earns it an appropriate common name: swamp maple.

At an enclosure ahead, owls await your inspection. These birds are keenly sensitive to sound. The barn owl best exemplifies the owl's highly developed auditory skills. In complete darkness, a barn owl can swiftly and accurately pounce on a running mouse. Controlled experiments have demonstrated that owls use only their ears for nocturnal hunting.

You may hear a sharp snapping noise as you near the barred owl's enclosure. This sound, made by the rapid opening and shutting of its beak, is part of the owl's threat display. Another of its "threatening" movements includes the "puffing out" of feathers to make it appear much larger than actual size.

Walk past the bridge over the Scantic River leading to the Big River Loop.

The apple tree at the next station provides a home for a family of black-capped chickadees. These pert birds also excavate cavities for nests in rotten birches or pine stumps. You can easily imitate their softly whistled *dee-dee* call. Hawks and eagles inhabit an enclosure on the right.

You may hear deer pulling at grass and clover as they

The Crooked Little Path

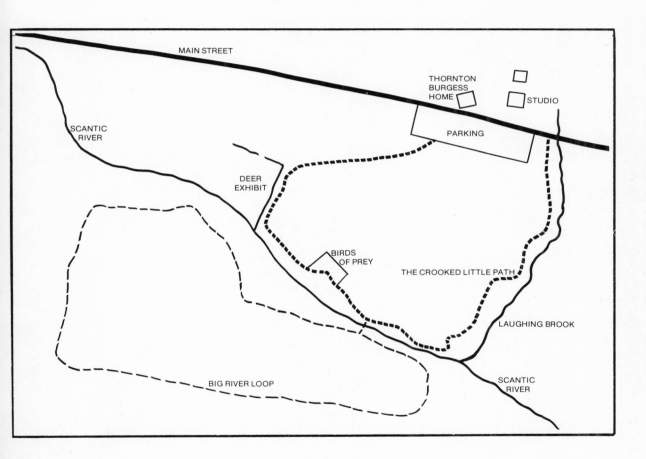

graze in the exhibit ahead to the left. If you place your open palm against the chain link fence, one of these white-tailed deer may come over to nuzzle your hand and lick the salt from it. Deer depend primarily on their noses to sense danger—or the salt perspiration leaves on your hand.

At the end of the deer pen you bear right along Great Meadow. Tree swallows nest in the elevated bird boxes here.

You'll recognize them by their sweet, liquid twitterings. Crickets also are meadow residents.

Continue along the guide rope to the completion of the loop trail at the parking lot.

Tree Swallow   **The Crooked Little Path**

The Stebbins Wildlife Refuge

28. The Stebbins Wildlife Refuge

Class: II
Distance (round trip): 1.8 miles
Hiking time: 1¼ hours

The Stebbins Wildlife Refuge is an excellent example of how lands can be preserved and maintained by interested people. Years ago, several members of Springfield's Allen Bird Club raised money and began buying land along the Connecticut River in Longmeadow for $25 an acre. As money became available, more land was purchased in this area known as Longmeadow Flats. Even though inflation has driven the per-acre price to $600, the club has continued to buy up and preserve what it can.

The refuge schedules an active year-round calendar of events. Bird banding demonstrations and nature walks led by local experts cover such subjects as mushrooms, trees, animal tracks, wild flowers, aquatic insects, and edible wild plants. Information about the yearly program, as well as a map of the refuge and pamphlet describing the self-guiding nature trail (15¢), can be obtained from the officers of the Allen Bird Club. Contact the Springfield Museum of Science for a list of their names.

Maidenhair fern

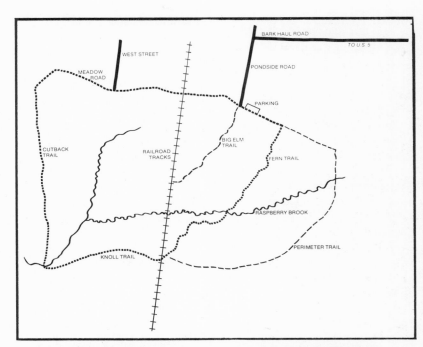

To reach this attractive, isolated region, drive south from the Springfield–Longmeadow line on US 5 (Longmeadow Street) for 2.4 miles. Turn right onto Bark Haul Road and follow it .4 miles to Pondside Road. Turn left and drive .4 miles to its end (and junction with Meadow Road). A large refuge sign stands partially hidden by trees directly across the road. You can park to the left near the guard rail.

This walk will follow the self-guiding nature trail (actually the Fern and Knoll Trails) and the Cutback Trail. To begin, walk left past the guard rail to the point where the old road widens a bit. You'll see two wooden posts flanking a grassy path on the right. Take this trail and follow the yellow blazes.

The appropriately named trail passes through ferns of more than fifteen varieties. One of the most interesting, and certainly one of the largest to watch for is the ostrich fern. Its fronds taper on both ends and grow to a length of five feet. This plant is a world traveler, growing from Virginia to the Arctic Circle in North America as well as in Europe and Asia.

Grasslike plants called sedges grow in the wet, sunny clearing near station 3. Their dying leaves help to build up this low area. Muskrats use them along with marsh grasses to build houses on shores or in shallow water.

The grassy path crosses two footbridges before becoming somewhat rootier. Often, heavy side growth closes around the trail, producing a "tunnel" effect which makes the rest of the world seem particularly distant.

One of the most beautiful birds you'll see in the refuge is the scarlet tanager. This is the only North American bird with a red body and black wings and tail. First-year males may be more orange than red. Females have small-er, darker bills and greenish yellow coloring.

The Fern Trail swings left as the Perimeter Trail joins from the left. Stay on the former. Cross the double railroad tracks (they are in use so be careful) and follow the yellow arrow straight and then sharply right. Now on the Knoll Trail, you wind back parallel to the tracks before swinging away from them through clusters of sumac.

The narrow dirt footpath passes open scrubland where hawks search for small rodents. The uplifted branches of red pine, planted by Allen Bird Club members, become more prominent as the trail climbs to the top of a hill. Below to the right the hillside slopes steeply down to a brook.

At a fork, the yellow blazes lead down a long grade to the right through striking, smooth-barked beeches. The damp path approaches the Connecticut River, swings right across a footbridge, and becomes the Cutback Trail. This wide, grassy road travels through lush greenery. Everywhere you look—from the grass at foot level, to the ferns alongside the trail, to shrubs and bushes at head level, and up to tree tops—green predominates.

Reaching a dirt turnaround, the Cutback Trail loses its silky footing and becomes a graveled road. It loops right, past a small meadow, to a gas line. West Street branches left here to bisect a large meadow. Keep straight on the dirt road. Climb a slight grade over old blacktop pavement to the railroad tracks. The dirt road across the tracks will return you to your car.

The Stebbins Wildlife Refuge

29. Mount Tom Reservation

Class: III
Elevation: 1,210 feet
Vertical rise: 1,480 feet
Distance (round trip): 8.2 miles
Hiking time: 5¼ hours

This long trek winds through the Mount Tom State Reservation's shady woods, beside the quiet waters of Lake Bray, and along the cliffs of the Mount Tom Range. Some of the most spectacular scenery described in this entire book unfolds below as you walk the Metacomet-Monadnock Trail over the trap rock cliffs. (You can shorten this outing to a 4-mile hike along the cliffs by climbing only the Metacomet-Monadnock Trail.)

Although difficult to imagine, 15,000-foot mountains once rose from the valley where Mount Tom pokes its 1,210-foot summit skyward. Frost and water eventually reduced those towering peaks to sea level plains. Erupting volcanoes then created Mount Tom and Mount Holyoke. A glacier smothered the entire area some 50,000 years ago and striated the trap rock so strikingly visible today.

To reach the start of this hike, drive to the Mount Tom State Reservation sign on US 5, located 3.5 miles north of the junction of route 5 and US 202 (north) in Holyoke and 4.2

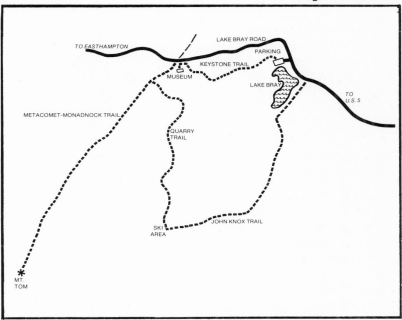

miles south of the intersection of route 5 and Mass 10 in Northampton. Turn west onto Lake Bray Road and follow it to the warming shelter just beyond Lake Bray. Park in front of the shelter. You'll want to bring water on this long trek. Fill canteens in the shelter's restrooms.

Walk back along Lake Bray Road to the far end of the guard rail at the water's edge. Turn right onto the John Knox Trail

(no sign). This flat, narrow dirt path follows orange blazes through thick woods along the east shore of the lake. Leaves interlock overhead to shield you from the sun's rays. Canada lilies fill the trail sides.

The path swings away from the pond and climbs gradually through hemlocks surrounded at root level by ground pine, ferns, and mountain laurel. After ¾ miles of hiking, the way swings sharply left and

Trap rock cliffs

At the 1-mile point turn left onto the intersecting path for 20 feet and then right at the orange blaze. Follow this trail approximately 100 feet to the edge of a grassy clearing (dotted with young trees) above US 91. Swing right onto the unsigned dirt trail and quickly left at the fork ahead. Continue straight on this route, ignoring the several dirt paths crossing and intersecting it. Keeping I-91 on the left, walk through sumac bushes to a trail junction marked by large orange blazes. Turn right here back into the woods.

At the fork ahead follow the orange blazes onto the dirt road at the right. This flat trail winds leisurely to a stream at the base of a grassy hill (the grass may not be beaten down enough to identify the trail). Climb straight up the hill and walk across the top to a gravel road. Go left.

As you enter the large parking area and approach ski development buildings, watch for the Quarry Trail on the right. This

climbs steeply to a hilltop. Shiny white birches sparkle in the hardwood forest as the trail levels out.

Mount Tom Reservation

old gravel road leads sharply back to the right, just before the chair lifts begin their crawl up the mountain. After 1.8 miles of hiking you climb the old road and loop around to the left. At the fork ahead, bear right to the flat area at the base of the quarry.

Swing sharply right onto the old road leading up along the quarry's edge. This road turns sharply left at the corner of the quarry. Continue straight here, entering the woods through openings in two snow fences. Cross two brooks and ascend the long, very gradual, rocky grade.

If one can judge by the droppings they leave, this trail is popular with area animals, possibly as a walkway connecting forest haunts. The scats along the way give clues about the type of animals which deposited them. Size, shape, and color provide initial identifying data. Berry seeds, grass, and hair found inside will help you further in reading these trail "signs."

The path levels out and becomes grassier and shady.

The footing turns to dirt as the way widens and reaches an intersection after 3 miles of hiking (directly across is a wood shed). Turn left here onto the white-blazed Metacomet-Monadnock Trail.

This 2-mile section of trail will take you to the summit of Mount Tom. It weaves in and out of cool forests, lingering at innumerable overlooks atop ledges. Automobile sounds drift up from far below as you follow the crest of the trap rock cliffs.

You'll cross two peaks (1,015-foot Whiting Peak and 1,100-foot Dead Top), climb up over many ledged outcroppings, and pass hundreds of blueberry bushes before reaching the summit. Once there, the partial views you've been seeing all along combine to form a sweeping south-to-north panorama. You look across tree and house tops to farmlands with mountains beyond. Tranquility softens the scene.

When ready, retrace your steps on the Metacomet-Monadnock Trail to the junction

with the Quarry Trail. Continue straight ¼ mile to Lake Bray Road and turn right. Just ahead is the Robert Cole Museum of Natural History. An interesting assortment of live and stuffed animals awaits your inspection here.

Continue ¼ mile east (right) on Lake Bray Road. Cross over a stream and take the next trail to the right. This unblazed, wide path (Keystone Trail) shortly swings left and ascends gradually. It makes a sudden swing to the left and reaches a fork. Go right onto the orange-blazed path. Occasional wooden "day camp" markers help guide you along the way. This trail winds steadily downhill, crosses a dried brook, and levels out between hemlocks.

Ferns swarm over the forest floor as the trail bends right to junction with another path. Turn left and walk to a parking area (Lake Bray can be seen through trees to the right). Go left again at the end of this lot and make your way to a second parking area. Cross over the small stone bridge to your car.

Mount Tom Reservation

Mount Holyoke

30. Mount Holyoke

Class: III
Elevation: 930 feet
Vertical rise: 825 feet
Distance (round trip): 2.75 miles
Hiking time: 1¾ hours

The prestigious old hotel on Mount Holyoke's summit has entertained such luminaries as Charles Dickens, Nathaniel Hawthorne, Jenny Lind, and Abraham Lincoln. The present building is smaller by sixty rooms, a ballroom, and dining room than it was prior to the mid-twentieth-century hurricane which inflicted heavy damage. Though no longer used as a food and drink establishment, its broad verandas attract many people because of their expansive views.

From its intersection with Mass 116, drive northwest on Mass 47 for 2.7 miles to the entrance of the Joseph Allen Skinner Park. Turn right and drive ½ mile to the summit road's wooden gate and looping turn. Park your car in one of the pull-off areas near this intersection.

Walk up the macadam summit road past sparkling birches and statuesque hemlocks. After ½ mile of hiking (just before the Halfway House clearing) you reach the brown and white sign, "To Summit,"

View from Mount Holyoke

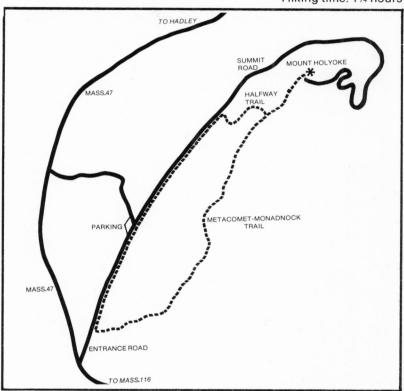

on the right. Turn here and begin the steep climb up the Halfway Trail.

Small rocks cobble the path and larger ones form steps up the slope through cool woods. Follow the path as it switches back to the left and continues to climb steep-

ly beside a line of hemlocks.

One of the most unusual trees you'll see on this route is the striped maple. Black and white lines streak its smooth, greenish bark.

After a series of short swings to the right and left, the Half-

Mount Holyoke

way Trail ends at the Metacomet-Monadnock Trail. Continue straight on this white-
blazed trail as it weaves
across level terrain and bends
left. Follow it up over spines
of ledge to Mount Holyoke's
summit.

You may be startled and then
awed by the views opening up
to the left. From this vantage
point you gaze west to north
across the looping Connecticut River. Power boats churn
the waters, leaving wide,
white scars. Beyond the river, patchwork farmlands and
clusters of suburban house-
tops sprawl to the bases of
rounded mountains. On ideal,
hazeless days, you can see
Mount Greylock to the northwest and Vermont's Mount
Ascutney to the north.

Climb up to the hotel's porch
for a four-sided view (only
the view to the northeast is
partially obscured by trees).
You may also see red-tailed
hawks circling easily on the
air currents. Watch them tuck
their wings and plummet swiftly earthward. The hawk's
dark belly band and tail color—
reddish above, buffy pink below

make identification easier.

Retrace your steps from the
summit to the Metacomet-
Monadnock Trail. Go straight
at the intersection where the
Halfway Trail branches right,
continuing to follow the white
blazes.

You come quickly to a hem-
lock-framed view of the Connecticut River Valley. This
is only the first of a series
of overlooks along the Metacomet-Monadnock Trail. Much
of your 1½-mile return route
on this trail includes short
ascents over ledged areas
alternating with quick descents
through wooded sections. Be
careful of the loose rocks
spilling across some parts
of the trail.

After passing beneath high
tension lines, the path drops
more steeply, soon meeting
an old road. Swing right onto
the road for about 100 feet
to where it intersects the
Skinner Park graveled en-
trance road. Turn right onto
the park road and hike the
½ mile back to your car.

Mount Holyoke

31. Arcadia Wildlife Sanctuary

Class: I
Distance (round trip): 1.8 miles
Hiking time: 1 hour

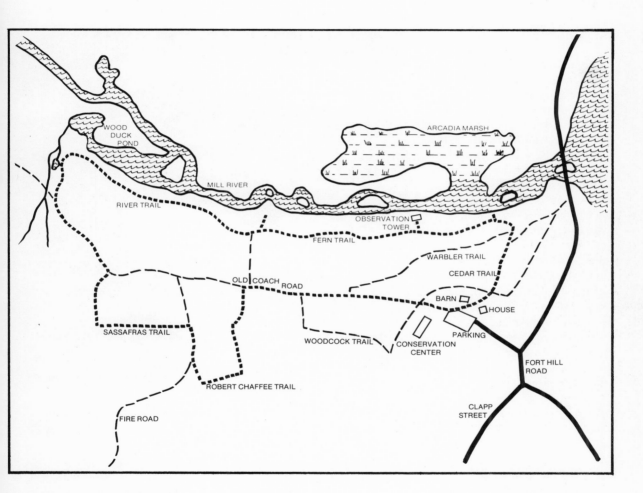

More than 500 acres of fields, woodlands, and marshes have been preserved at the Arcadia Wildlife Sanctuary in Easthampton. Attempts are underway to raise the thousands of dollars necessary to expand the sanctuary by purchasing additional land along this oxbow of the Connecticut River. Sanctuary personnel offer scheduled, guided tours and a summer day camp. A conservation center adds an educational dimension to the natural areas.

Free admission to the sanctu-

Wood Duck

ary is granted Massachusetts Audubon Society members, residents of Easthampton and Northampton, bicyclists, pedestrians, and visitors to the Watershed Council. If you don't fit into any of the above categories, the charges are: $1. per auto or motorcycle and $10. per bus. The trails are open from sunrise to sunset, every day of the year.

Take exit 18 off I-95 and drive south on US 5 for 1.3 miles. Turn right onto East Street and follow it 1.2 miles to Fort Hill Road. Turn right again. The sanctuary entrance is .7 miles down this road on the left (just beyond the junction with Clapp Street).

To begin this circuit route, walk behind the row of trees along the parking area's right side. The Cedar Trail begins just to the left of the large white house. Sumacs, cedars, locusts, and a variety of other shrubs and trees (some labeled to make identification easier) line this flat path. Bird houses merge inconspicuously with the leaves.

At a large, grassy clearing, follow the second path to the left. Now on the Fern Trail, you walk the shady, dirt path past purple-flowering raspberry bushes. This shrub has large, unmistakable, maple-shaped leaves. Both leaves and stems are hairy, but the stems do not have spines as other raspberries do.

Watch on the right for the observation tower. This inviting structure has a spiral metal staircase winding to the elevated tower. From this high vantage point you can survey the Arcadia Marsh. Although early morning and late afternoon are the best times, you may see wildlife activity at any hour.

Arcadia Wildlife Sanctuary

Pass an overlook to the right and climb the stone steps to an intersection. Continue straight across onto the River Trail. Occasional roots and dips in this narrow path make the going a bit rougher than that of the flat Cove and Fern trails.

Red baneberry cluster to the right of the path. This shrub, one to two feet high, likes shaded woodlands and thickets near streams. Tiny white flowers form dense clusters at stem ends, and are replaced by clusters of half-inch poisonous red berries, each with a black dot at its end. Edging closer to the water, the River Trail approaches Wood Duck Pond and switches back to the left. The many large wooden bird houses along this trail and across the pond are actually wood-duck boxes. They serve as substitute homes for this multi-colored duck which normally nests in tree hollows. The modern forestry practice of removing dried or diseased trees has deprived wood ducks of their natural nesting sites. The wood duck population has shown

a dramatic recovery as their man-made homes have become more numerous.

Green herons frequent the wet area beside the trail's switchback. Although several species of heron occupy the open water of the marsh and pond, they never compete for available food. The short-legged green heron often watches from overhanging branches for aquatic animal life. The blackcrowned night heron fishes at night in shallow waters. The great blue heron, with head hunched on shoulders, stalks prey in the shallows.

Turn left at the next intersection and climb the short, steep hill. This long straight path contains several muddy sections, ideal areas for print watching. You'll see human, horse, and other animal tracks along here.

Turn right onto the Sassafras Trail. This narrow, needle-covered path has a softer atmosphere as it winds through young tree growth. Along the way are the trees which give the trail its name.

Go left at the next trail intersection and right at the T intersection where a sign for the Chafee Trail points left. In 1944, Harvard College Professor and Mrs. Zachariah Chafee, Jr., donated Arcadia to the Massachusetts Audubon Society in memory of their son, Robert S. Chafee, for whom this trail was named.

Go left at the fork ahead, passing beneath overhanging hemlock boughs. The flat, pleasant trail passes a bench overlooking the Birch Swamp.

At the next intersection go left. Thick stands of eastern white pine litter the trail with needles and long, slender cones. Drop down a short, sandy embankment to a five-way intersection. Keeping the logs and planks atop a muddy area to the right, walk straight ahead onto Old Coach Road and up the slight grade.

This wider trail passes through thick ground cover of wild lily of the valley dotted with pink lady's slippers. Continue straight, past the Warbler Trail branching left, back to the parking area.

Arcadia Wildlife Sanctuary

At the Arcadia Wildlife
Sanctuary in Easthampton,
a child (or an adult, for that
matter) can scooch down
and sniff noses with Woodrow
Woodchuck and gaze eyeball
to eyeball with a great horned
owl. There may be baby wood
ducks available for close inspection or you may hear the
snorting sound of the bandit-
masked raccoon. The animals
caged and cared for at the
sanctuary would not be able to
survive in the wild because
they had been injured or had
become dependent upon human
beings. Mounted specimens
and three-dimensional displays in the conservation center allow close examination
and exploration of animal
anatomy and land topography.

By exploring along the Duckling Nature Trail, you will
have a chance to see animals
and plants in their natural
habitat. This trail was designed especially for children—and anyone else still
young in spirit. Step softly,
sharpen your eyes, and stretch
your ears.

Directions to the Arcadia

Wildlife Sanctuary appear in
Hike 31. Walk from the parking lot along Old Coach Road
past the conservation center
on the left. (Pamphlets with

explanations keyed to the nature trail's numbered stations
are available in the center's
lobby.) After 200 feet you'll
see a sign for the Warbler

Duckling Nature Trail

32. Duckling Nature Trail

Class: I
Distance (round trip): .5 miles
Hiking time: ½ hour

Tadpole

Trail on the right. Turn here. Look for the Duckling Nature Trail's yellow-numbered wooden posts along this route.

Station 4 acquaints you with gray birch trees. Black, triangular patches highlight the chalky white bark. It is easy to confuse this tree with the white birch. However, its bark has a duskier look and does not peel as easily as that of its better known cousin. (Incidentally, leave the bark on the trees; tearing it off can permanently disfigure an older tree—and may kill a younger one.)

Look to the north from station 6 for a view of the Mount Tom Range. This side of the range is a migratory flyway for thousands of hawks in the spring and fall.

Reptiles and amphibians reside in the marsh beyond station 8. Amphibians include frogs, toads, and salamanders. Snakes and turtles are reptiles. These "cold-blooded" animals hibernate during the winter. Basking in

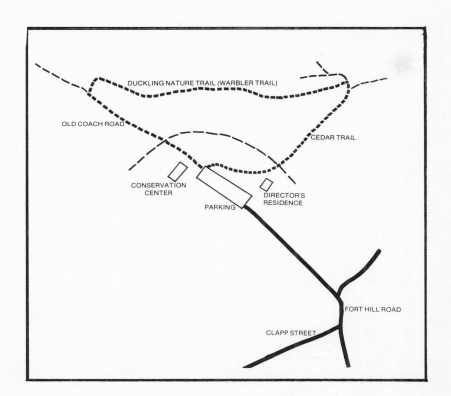

the sun on summer days helps speed up their body functions. Herons and raccoons feed on them all.

The unusual shagbark hickory grows near station 9. Identify mature trees by their gray bark hanging like paper streamers. Smooth, gray bark covers the young trees.

A briar patch near station 12 (as well as the brush pile at station 2) is a haunt favored by the cottontail rabbit.

Turn right beyond the large hemlock at station 17 onto the grassy path. A short walk will bring you past the enclosed animals to the parking area.

Western Massachusetts

View from Pine Cobble

Chesterfield Gorge

The Gorge

Waters of the Westfield River East Branch boil between Chesterfield Gorge's sheer ledge walls. Centuries of liquid force have scooped pockets in ledge and boulder faces. Atop the steep sides of this river-hewn chasm hemlocks find rootholds and frame the more tranquil downstream views beyond. A conical, stone-faced bridge pier rises at the gorge's upper edge; it is the sole reminder of civilization in the chasm's primitive depths.

From Mass 143, just west of the West Chesterfield Bridge, turn south onto River Road. After .8 miles, turn left onto the road indicated by the Chesterfield Gorge sign. Follow this short dirt road to the Trustees of Reservations parking area. The parking fee is 25¢ on weekdays and $1 on weekends.

Walk left of the small red and white building to the left of the parking lot. Descend the dirt path through the woods, cross an old road, and walk

33. Chesterfield Gorge

Class: II
Distance (along gorge and back): .5 miles
Hiking time: ½ hour

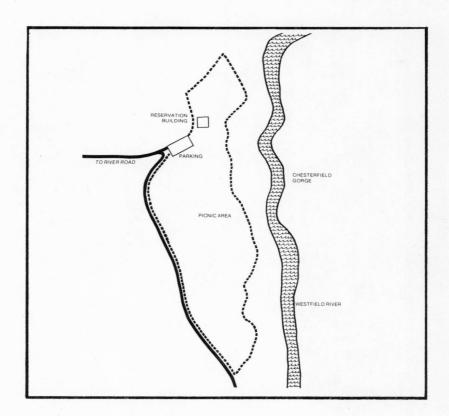

to the water's edge. From here you can see the river as it makes a sweeping bend before it swirls through the natural channel ahead.

Swing right, following alongside the steel-cable fence (it parallels your entire route beside the gorge). Look across the river to the old Boston-Albany Post Road's remaining bridge support.

Climb steeply back up behind the reservation building (the cable fence provides helpful support). Though you are out of sight of the gorge at times, the river's rushing, surging road accompanies you throughout the hike.

The trail winds along above the gorge which allows for intermittent views. You'll see glacial boulders above and beside the way. You can look down into the gorge to where the water churns around scarred and gouged glacial masses. Submerged rocks tear the river's surface.

The trail continues to wind gradually beside the fence paralleling the gorge. Wood-chips have been sprinkled over these elevated sections to make the walking more comfortable. After passing through the last rock funnel, the river slows. Froth flecks its now more peaceful surface.

Mountain laurel edges the trail just before it rises to meet the road at the end of the fence.

You can return to your car by turning right onto the road and following it back to the parking lot or by retracing your steps on the path high above the gorge. Either way, you'll pass picnic tables nestled beneath towering hemlocks. A box lunch could extend your stay in this ruggedly appealing setting.

Chesterfield Gorge

34. Dorothy Frances Rice Sanctuary

Class: II
Distance (round trip): 1.7 miles
Hiking time: 1 hour

The Dorothy Frances Rice Sanctuary for Wildlife in Peru is charming. The effect was not achieved without effort. Manicured grounds near the visitors' center accent the wildness of surrounding forests. Flower beds sparkle against the greens of grass and forest. The rustic visitors' center provides a restful atmosphere for browsing through information about local animals and sanctuary history and its round, wooden table map of the sanctuary adds a craftsmanlike touch to the scene.

Easy-to-follow color-coded trails wind through 273 acres of woodland. The paths are cleared and mowed for comfortable walking, but bordering areas have been left natural to attract and support wildlife. Because the area is devoted to animals, visitors are asked to stay on the trails and leave by sundown. The sanctuary remains open daily except Tuesday from May 28 to October 18. For group nature-study walks and

Cottontail Rabbit

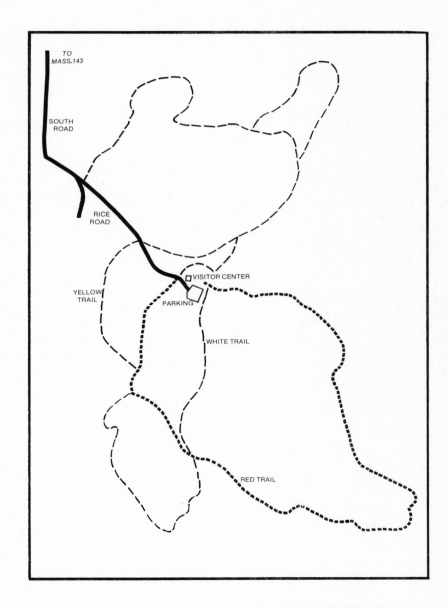

Dorothy Frances Rice Sanctuary

snowshoe outings make reservations with the superintendent.

From Mass 143 in the town of Peru, drive 1 mile south on South Road to the sanctuary entrance. Follow signs to the parking area.

The Red Trail, longest of the sanctuary's paths, begins almost directly across Rice Road from the visitors' center. The wide, grassy path passes between berry bushes and fruit trees which provide abundant food for area wildlife. Passing the exiting yellow trail (on the right), the path descends gradually.

Crossing over the intersecting White Trail, the way continues to descend easily. Stone walls begin to appear. The frequency with which they parallel or cross the Red Trail will increase as you continue on. Imagine what this land was once like after it had been cleared of rocks for subsistence farming by early settlers.

Red arrows guide you at turns and intersections, while red blazes mark the route at other times. You begin a long gradual climb through fern-filled woods. The density of earlier vegetation has disappeared; grass has given way to dead twigs and leaves. Walking becomes noisier; your chances of seeing wildlife decrease.

However, you might surprise a cottontail rabbit crouched in the middle of the path with ears up, nose twitching, and eyes wide with watchfulness before it bounds away.

Watch for weasel footprints in damp areas both on the trail and beside brooks. These creatures are bold, persistent hunters which explore in leaps and bounds while searching for prey. They store food for future use, often piling up a heap of dead mice in a concealed spot near their dens. Their scats are long and slender, dark brown or black in color, and usually contain fur and bones. Because weasels repeatedly use the same area, you'll see accumulations of their droppings along the trail or atop stone walls. When disturbed, they emit a charactertistic odor almost as strong as that of a skunk.

Continue to follow the red blazes over flat paths and gradual inclines, beside stone walls, across trickling brooks, and through hardwood forests. You'll climb up through evergreens just before walking into the clearing next to your car.

Dorothy Frances Rice Sanctuary

35.   Notchview Reservation

Class: II
Elevation: 2,297 feet
Vertical rise: 390 feet
Distance (round trip): 4.4 miles
Hiking time: 2½ hours

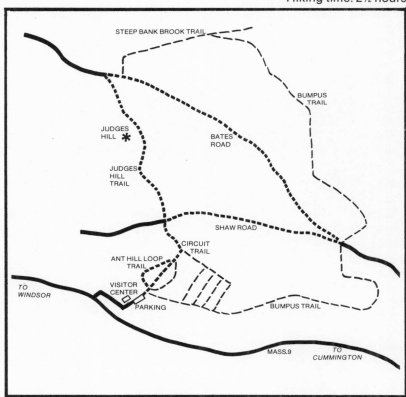

An interesting network of trails and old country roads crisscross the 3,000 acres of wooded hillsides and old hayfields at Notchview Reservation in Windsor. Most of the land, part of the Hoosac Range, is more than 1,900 feet high.

On Mass 9, drive 3.4 miles west from the Cummington-Windsor line or 1 mile east from the junction of routes 9 and 8A in Windsor. Turn north at the Notchview Reservation sign and follow similar signs into the first driveway on the left. There is ample parking across from the visitors' center. Hiking, snowshoeing, crosscountry skiing, and picnicking are encouraged within the reservation; motorized vehicles are prohibited.

Follow the sign "to trails" north from the parking lot between white fences. At the trail junction ahead, bear sharply left onto the yellow-blazed Ant Hill Loop. Keep left at a second junction just ahead.

After crossing a brook, this wide, bumpy trail leads gradually uphill between aromatic spruce and balsam. Miniature forests of shining clubmoss thrive underfoot. Its erect, six-inch stems support sharp-tipped leaves which are, appropriately, both shining and green. The plant favors the rich, acidic soils of moist woods.

Bear right at the partially-hidden T intersection. To the left of the grassy trail is a flourishing colony of low bush blueberries. The trail narrows and enters fern-filled woods before passing through a darkened spruce glen.

Go left at the T intersection onto the Circuit Trail. You

Notchview Reservation

quickly reach still another T intersection. Go left here onto Judges Hill Trail. This wide grassy lane soon crosses graveled Shaw Road. Continue across this road, following the sign for Judges Hill Trail into the woods. The lush, ankle-level undergrowth teems with self heal, whose purple, two-lipped flowers grow in a terminal spike. Early herbalists, who used self heal for curing sore throats and other minor ailments, gave the plant its common name.

Yellow blazes continue to guide you along this trail. Blackberry bushes tear at your legs or pants, but if it's late summer they reimburse you for the trouble with their fruit. Cross a small brook atop old wooden logs and pick your way over several boggy sections.

The trail begins a gradual, then steeper, ascent toward the summit of Judges Hill (2,297 feet). Smooth gray beech trees march in columns beside the trail.

Notchview Reservation Entrance

Soon you reach the unmarked, viewless summit of Judges Hill. An old foundation remains beside the trail; stones define its perimeter and rise to form a dilapidated chimney. This was the home of one of the two dozen families who farmed the land now comprising the reservation. The area's typically New England, rocky soil and abbreviated growing season proved economically hazardous for those early settlers. They gradually found lumbering and livestock raising to be more secure and profitable.

Beyond the Judges Hill summit, the trail descends through more beech forests. After 1.6 miles it emerges onto Bates Road, an old stage coach route. Turn right here and follow the yellow blazes along the road. This route bears the name of Herman L. "Butter" Bates. He was known in the area for his high quality butter and also had the distinction of bringing the first white flour to Windsor.

Stone walls occasionally border this long, level stretch of road. The air smells clean.

Bates Road bends right and descends gradually to an angled intersection with Shaw Road after 3 miles of hiking. Turn sharp right. Follow the rising grade as the trail winds between thick woodlands. At 3.8 miles you reach the spot where you originally crossed Shaw Road on the Judges Hill Trail.

Swing left into the woods, retracing your earlier route. Turn right onto the first side trail and continue past the Ant Hill Loop Trail. You are now on the yellow-blazed Circuit Trail.

Evergreens spill their needles onto the path, giving it a cushioned feel. Leaving the conifers, the grassy path descends gradually to the junction with the start of the Ant Hill Loop after 4.4 miles of hiking. Walk ahead, between the white fences, to your car.

Notchview Reservation

36.   Borden Mountain

Class: II
Elevation: 2,506 feet
Vertical rise: 406 feet
Distance (round trip): 2.8 miles
Hiking time: 1½ hours

Thousands of acres of unmolested woodlands swarm over the countryside below. Scattered farms outnumber visible cities. Rolling mountaintops rise above, as if to protect the scenic wilderness. Vermont? New Hampshire? Maine? No—Massachusetts! This 360-degree view from the fire tower atop Borden Mountain is a thrilling sight any time of year but particularly in the fall. Try climbing up on a day when the skies are clear and you can gaze across the treetops to the distant horizons.

From the white church in Savor, drive 500 feet west on Mass 116 to the Savoy Mountain State Forest sign. Turn north on Center Road 2.8 miles to its end. Turn right onto Adams Road. Drive 1.1 miles to a fork marked by a fern-filled triangle supporting four evergreens. Park anywhere along the roadside in this area.

The route to Borden Mountain begins on graveled Bannis Road, leading right from the triangle. The initial climb is a steady,

Mushrooms

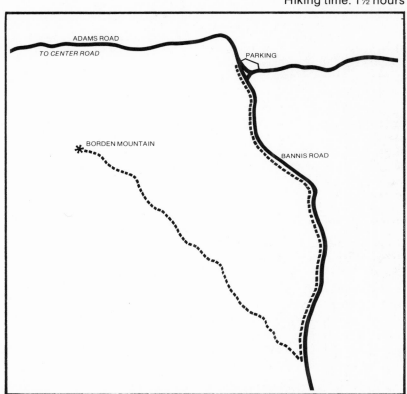

moderate one. The road levels as it passes through thick woods. Striped maples droop their huge three-lobed leaves over the tops of ferns proliferating at ground level. The walking is flat and shady.

Descending gradually, Bannis Road crosses Horseford

Brook and enters woods blackened by the skeletal forms of towering white spruces. Only the uppermost sections of these trees receive enough sunlight to keep their needles green.

The road rises to reach the narrow path leading to Bor-

Borden Mountain

den Mountain after ¾ of a mile. A widened grassy area to the right leads quickly to the dirt footpath. Evergreen spills cover its surface; grasses line the edges.

A huge, quartz-streaked glacial boulder is to the right at the 1 mile point. The trail widens, taking on the appearance of an old road. Low-running blackberries abound in and beside the way.

Rising over boulders imbedded in the dirt, the path funnels through lines of closely-packed evergreens. Ahead, fireweed thrusts its four-foot spires above the grasses. Its lavender blossoms top slender, oblong pods. As its name implies, fireweed grows abundantly on burned-over ground.

Wade through blackberry bushes to the clearing at the base of the Walker Lookout Tower. The views are blocked at this level by a circle of trees; you'll have to climb the tower. (The tower itself is locked, but the upper steps afford a prime view.)

You can look up and down the mountains edging the western border of the state. Look south-southwest for the prominent fire tower on Mount Everett. Southwest and closer is the Lenox Mountain fire tower. Brodie Mountain, also bearing a fire tower, is almost due west, while Mount Greylock raises its highest-in-Massachusetts summit and tower just west of north. The lower end of Vermont's green Mountain chain can be seen to the north; Hogback Mountain sits silhouetted to the northeast. The low hills of central Massachusetts complete the view to the east.

When ready, return by the same route to your car.

Borden Mountain

37.   Spruce Hill (Mount Busby)

Class: III
Elevation: 2,566 feet
Vertical rise: 681 feet
Distance (round trip): 2.6 miles
Hiking time: 1½ hours

The chances of savoring wild berries are very favorable if you ascend this peak in July or August. You needn't be too precise: if you miss the red raspberries near the bottom, there are always the blackberries which mature later farther up. And if you're too early for the blackberries, blueberries await you at the summit.

This hike's appeal does not rest solely upon its wild edibles. Most of the journey is pleasantly invigorating; just demanding enough to warm up your muscles, but not so punishing that it drains your vitality. Once you've reached the top, splendid views will reward your efforts.

Spruce Hill seems to be as common a name for Massachusetts mountains as Bald Mountain is for Vermont peaks. This particular Spruce Hill is also known as Mount Busby (to help distinguish it from nearby Spruce Hill No. 2 and dual-peaked Spruce Hill: all three are located within Savoy Mountain State Forest).

To reach the start of the Busby

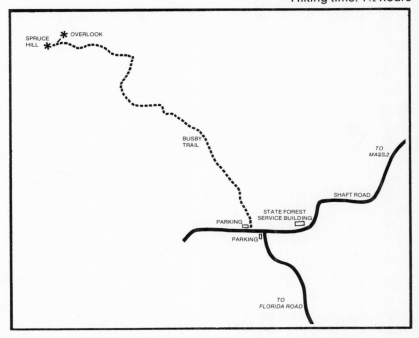

Trail, drive .4 miles east from the North Adams-Florida line on Mass 2 to the Savoy State Forest sign. Turn south (right) onto Shaft Road. Travel 2.8 miles, following signs to North Pond Recreation Area, to the State Forest Service building on the right. The trail begins at the next bend in Shaft Road. Park along the widened sides of the blacktop road (or, if your vehicle has high clearance, try the dirt road for a more

private spot).

Walk 150 feet west on the dirt road to a junction. Turn right and follow the blue triangular markers of the Busby Trail. The first of the promised berries appears shortly ahead.

The Busby Trail passes under a transmission line and enters thick woods. The road through the woods dampens and becomes boggy in places;

Spruce Hill (Mount Busby)

many logs lie scattered across the mud, supporting the trail. Rising slightly, the way reaches a second transmission swath and narrows to enter the woods beyond.

Ascending gradually, the path winds first through spruce then through hardwood forests. Occasional white birches accent the trail as grass creeps in. Staples Brook gurgles its way below the hillside to the right.

Rusty-hoof fomes (shaped like ant hills) grow on dead trees (primarily birches and beeches) along the trail. This perennial shelf fungus may grow for thirty-five years, adding a new zone of tubes each year. It was used by early settlers as tinder and punk.

Crossing a two-pronged brook at ¾ mile, the path leads up through wild ginger. The two heart-shaped leaves of this long-stemmed plant makes its identification unmistakable. The wild ginger root is used for medicinal purposes and as a spice.

Busby Trail

An old, large stone wall crawls down the hillside from the left, stopping abruptly at trail's edge. The trail climbs up over wet sections of flat rocks and ledge.

Ahead on the right, an old cellar foundation sinks into the hillside. Constructed with neither mortar nor cement, its six-foot-high sides of layered stones once supported an early settler's home. Even the rock-lined cellar stairway remains intact.

Blackberries lean over the path ahead as it switches back to the left at the 1 mile point. The grade increases; roots form a web along the trail. This final ¼ mile over steep, ledged sections will make you sweat even on cold days.

Just below the summit an overlook leads right (east). Both the view and the blueberries will draw you onto the bare-ledged outcropping. Continue left the few feet to Spruce Hill's summit.

The Hoosic River Valley extends north to south below. Look northwest (right) across Windsor Lake and North Adams to lower Green Mountain peaks. New York State's Taconics loom to the west-northwest and Mount Greylock rises above the valley just south of west. Looking down the valley to the southwest you see, beyond the town of Adams, Lakes Pontoosuc and Onota (in Pittsfield). Farther still, Mount Everett's pointed summit swells along the horizon. To the southeast, the fire tower atop Borden Mountain stands in solitude above wavy hilltops.

When filled with scenery (and probably berries as well), return to your car by the Busby Trail.

Spruce Hill (Mount Busby)

38. Raycroft Lookout

Class: II
Distance (to lookout and back): .6 miles
Hiking time: 20 minutes

As a consequence of the Depression and Franklin Roosevelt's belief that every boy (we would add every girl, too) should have a chance to work in the woods, the bare ledges of Raycroft Lookout boast an impressive stone balcony—courtesy of the Civilian Conservation Corps. A surprisingly-brief hike leads to this stone-walled vantage point which affords a dizzying aerial view of the Deerfield River Gorge and of nearby peaks. Two overlooks just off the trail offer additional westerly views.

Half a mile south of Whitcomb Summit on Mass 2, turn east onto Whitcomb Hill Road. (A brown and white sign here advertises Monroe State Forest and Lookout.) At the first sharp turn, continue straight ahead on Monroe Road (Whitcomb Hill Road bears right here). After descending to cross Fife Brook, keep straight on Raycroft Road (no signs here). At the height of land, 2.2 miles from route 2, turn right and drive the short distance to the parking area atop Hunt

View from Raycroft Lookout

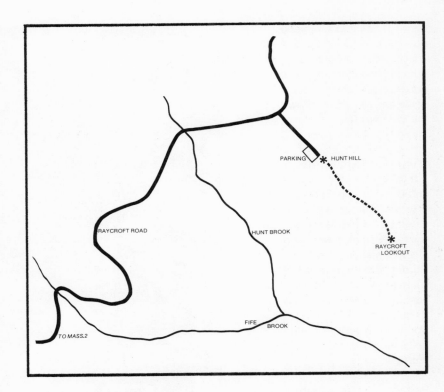

Hill. A sign at the far end of the parking lot marks the beginning of the trail.

The wide trail covered with woodchips descends gradually through stately, steel-gray beeches. Nearly all clothespins are made from this tree's strong, close-grained wood. Deer, bear, and other animals as well as birds feast on the edible kernels of its triangular nuts.

Watch for the two overlooks to the right (from the first one you can see Mount Greylock's rounded cone). Benches encourage a stop and some "wilderness" meditation before you continue to the Lookout.

You now hike over level ground

beneath hemlocks. A steep descent over steps banked with railroad ties marks your approach to Raycroft Lookout. Blueberries and white and red clover crowd the last few steps of path leading to the balcony.

Step out onto Raycroft Lookout for the heralded view. Far above the Deerfield River, rounded hilltops lead to higher summits. Brodie Mountain (and fire tower) dominates the skyline to the southwest (right). Borden Mountain rises highest to the south. To the southeast, Adams Mountain lifts its head at the end of a long ridgeline. Toad Mountain, just east of Adams, completes the view.

Retrace your steps to the parking lot atop Hunt Hill.

Blackening Russula

Raycroft Lookout

39. Pine Cobble

Class: III
Elevation: 1,894 feet
Vertical rise, 1, 164 feet
Distance (round trip): 2.8 miles
Hiking time: 1½ hours

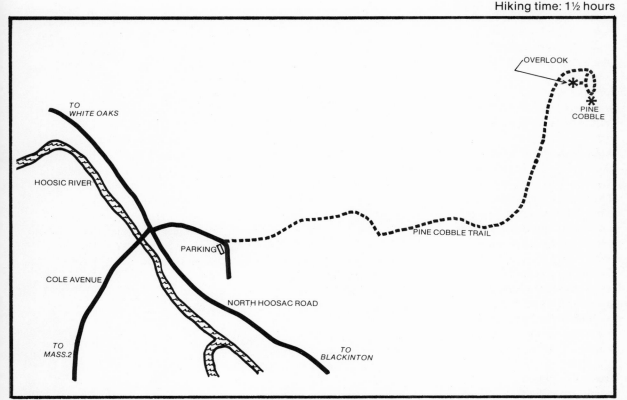

You can ascend the Pine Cobble Trail in less than an hour and relish a vista which includes Mount Williams, Mount Greylock, the Taconics in New York state, and the towns of North Adams and Williamstown. To catch this view at its best, wait for a clear day with picture-perfect clouds.

From US 2, 1.3 miles west of the North Adams-Williamstown line, turn north (right) onto Cole Avenue. Drive over the Hoosic River bridge and diagonally across North Hoosac Road onto the narrow gravel road leading up between houses. After ¼ mile on this road, park in the small cleared area on the right (just

beyond a bend). A white-lettered blue sign marks the start of the Pine Cobble Trail on the east (left) side of the road.

Blue blazes guide you along the path. Soon, the trail's incline and your straining muscles attest to the rapid gain in elevation. Thick stands of young trees, their branches meeting overhead, crowd the waysides; only fragments of sunlight pierce their curtain.

Listen and watch for the downy woodpecker. With the red patch on the back of its head it resembles the larger hairy woodpecker but has a shorter beak.

The trail continues to climb after crossing a rutted dirt road with a few downed trees to interrupt your progress.

Emetic russula mushrooms grow occasionally beside the path. Firm white stalks (one to three inches high) support disc-shaped caps. The reddish tops peel easily away from the gills beneath. Emetic russulas are poisonous ("emetic" comes from the Greek word for "vomit"). Identifying species of mushrooms and fungi is especially difficult; only experts should attempt to determine their edibility.

At .6 miles the trail crosses another woods road. Just ahead a trail enters from the right. Follow the light blue blazes upward to the left.

A rockslide route between tiers of ledge awaits you after ¾ miles of hiking. Take your time with the rough terrain and steep pitch here. When you've topped the ledge, turn around for a look at some Taconic peaks to the west.

A flat, narrow, rock-encrusted trail leads up from the ledge. After winding through trees the path enters a small clearing, crossing over bare ledge.

A final ½ mile of steady climbing brings you to a trail junction at 1.3 miles. A brown and white sign directs you right toward Pine Cobble.

Now heading along the ridge, the trail splits briefly, rejoining on the summit's convoluted ledge. This bare rock provides a vantage point for the promised views.

The body of water southward is the Mount Williams Reservoir; Mount Williams rises behind it. Due south you look up to Mount Greylock. The

Taconics spread out in the west. North Adams sets below to the southeast; Williamstown lies to the southwest.

Retracing your steps from Pine Cobble, turn quickly left (west) and walk out onto an overlook. From this grassy outcrop you can better see the Taconics and more of Williamstown.

Return to the Pine Cobble Trail and follow it back to your car.

View from Pine Cobble

Pine Cobble

40. Mount Williams

Class: III
Elevation: 2,951 feet
Vertical rise: 631 feet
Distance (round trip): 1.4 miles
Hiking time: 1 hour

This short, invigorating climb to the summit of Mount Williams sharpens your appetite and then provides a quiet, scenic spot where a trail lunch can restore your energy. You'll want to be prepared for a good workout. The persistent uphill climb varies little. Frequent rest stops will allow you to reach the top hungry enough for lunch, yet lively enough to enjoy the setting.

Drive to Notch Road on Mass 2 (it's either 2 miles west of the junction of routes 2 and 8 in North Adams, or 2.1 miles east of the North Adams-Williamstown line). Turn south onto Notch Road and follow it 4.5 miles to the pull off area at the Appalachian Trail crossing. A brown and white sign across the road points "to summit (Mount Greylock's)—three miles." The trail to Mount Williams starts here.

The white blazes lead over level ground between stands of straight red spruces. At shoulder level, young, bushy,

Red Squirrel

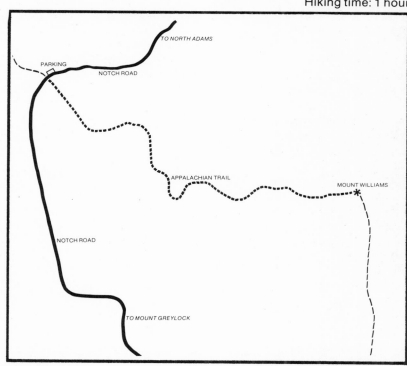

TO NORTH ADAMS

PARKING

NOTCH ROAD

APPALACHIAN TRAIL

MOUNT WILLIAMS

NOTCH ROAD

TO MOUNT GREYLOCK

spruces vie for sunlight. Lily of the valley spreads across the forest floor.

Winding gradually upward, the trail passes through stands of yellow birches. These handsome trees lack the striking appearance of their cousin, the paper birch, but have a unique yellowish-bronze coloration. On young-

er trees, the bark peels horizontally into narrow, curled strips.

The gutted trail climbs more steeply over rocks and roots. It swings sharply left after ¼ mile and continues its rough, ragged route. The loose rocks and gouges in the trail seem held together by the labyrinthine roots crisscrossing the way. Used as steps they make the ascent a bit easier.

The path is cheered by the presence of the fragile, clover-like common wood sorrel.

Rocks of white quartz highlight the trail as it assumes the appearance of a rock-and-root waterfall. After .6 miles of climbing the path levels out, narrows, and leads over a damp area. A short distance ahead you suddenly step out onto the ledged summit of Mount Williams.

The view, framed by trees, looks to the north and east across the town of North Adams. Rolling mountains form the backdrop. Most of the peaks stretching before you are in Vermont.

The Dome (2,748 feet) is closest to the left. Prospect Mountain (2,767 feet) is a bit right and farther back. Behind these two, Glastenbury Mountain raises its distant 3,748-foot head. Mount Snow (3,556 feet) and Haystack

Mountain (3,420 feet) fill the center (northeast) view in the distance while 2,415-foot Mount Olga can be seen more to the right.

Return by the same route to your car.

Mount Williams

41. Mount Prospect

Class: II
Elevation: 2,690 feet
Vertical rise: 422 feet
Distance (round trip): 2.6 miles
Hiking time: 1¼ hours

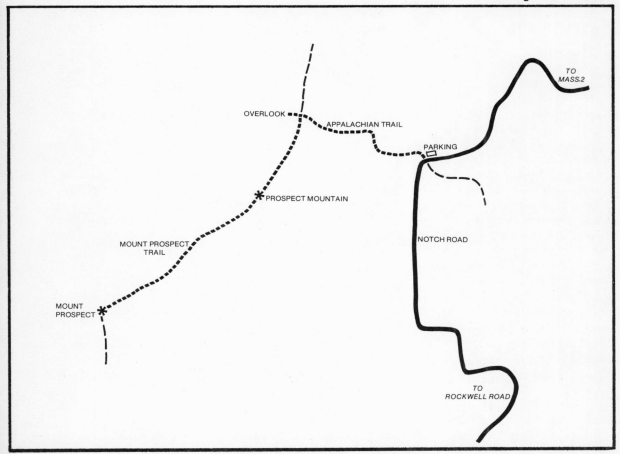

Mount Greylock Reservation, site of this hike to Mount Prospect, is located in Adams. The town, named in honor of Sam Adams of Revolutionary War fame, was split in 1878 into Adams and North Adams. In dividing, however, the original town lost none of the spunk so characteristic of its namesake. In 1920 North Adams displayed a sign celebrating the opening of the Mohawk Trail: "This is the City of North Adams, the Mother of the Mohawk Trail." Not to be outdone, Adams townfolk erected a sign at the border:

Mount Prospect

"You are now leaving Adams, the Mother of North Adams and the Grandmother of the Mohawk Trail."

To locate the start of the trail to Mount Prospect, refer to directions for Hike 40. Park in the suggested area.

At the brown and white sign pointing to Money Brook and Prospect Hill, walk north along the rutted road, following the Appalachian Trail. Keep right, guided by the trail's white, rectangular blazes.

Skeletal spruces fill the woods. Tunnel your way through younger, bushier spruces ahead. The trail levels, then begins gradually climbing over terrain roughened by rocks and roots.

Downed trees along the trail may host blackening russula. The mushroom's circular, concave, three- to six-inch cap turns brown or black. Old caps host smaller gill fungi.

Climbing more steeply, you

Silver-bordered Fritillary

step over ledge streaked with quartz. The path ducks between columns of spruces. Look back over your shoulder on some of the more elevated sections for a near view of Mount Williams.

Some spruce trunks support blister lichen, a grayish, leaf-like plant which grows where the air is unpolluted. Two kinds of plants, a fungus and an alga, make up a lichen. The fungus captures rainwater and supplies the alga with both water and minerals. Through photosynthesis, the alga provides carbohydrates for itself and the fungus.

At .4 miles you reach the junction with the Mount Prospect Trail. The Appalachian Trail swings north-northeast (right) here. Pause to enjoy a limited overlook to the northwest before turning left onto the blue-blazed path to Mount Prospect.

The way winds along the ridgeline. Look left and right for glimpses of companion peaks. Following a mild descent, the fern-bordered trail climbs easily. At approximately .7

miles you reach a grassy overlook marking the 2,582-foot summit of Prospect Mountain. (Yes, en route to Mount Prospect, you climb over Prospect Mountain!)

Beyond the crest of Prospect Mountain the trail rises gradually. Blackberry and raspberry bushes, wood asters, and hobblebush throttle the path, almost obliterating it in places. The hobblebush, with its large leaves, is particularly distinctive. White flowers appear in striking clusters in May or early June. Bright red fruit darkens to ebony at maturity. In winter, deer browse the shrub for its twigs and buds.

You walk into the shrub-enclosed clearing at Mount Prospect's summit after 1.3 miles of hiking. Dead trees offer prime habitat for the white-breasted nuthatch with its extraordinary habit of creeping down tree trunks head first. Listen for the nasal *yank* calls.

Return to Notch Road by the same route.

Mount Prospect

Mount Greylock

Sunset from Mount Greylock

42.   Mount Greylock

Class: IV
Elevation: 3,491 feet
Vertical rise: 2,491 feet
Distance (round trip): 6.1 miles
Hiking time: 4¼ hours

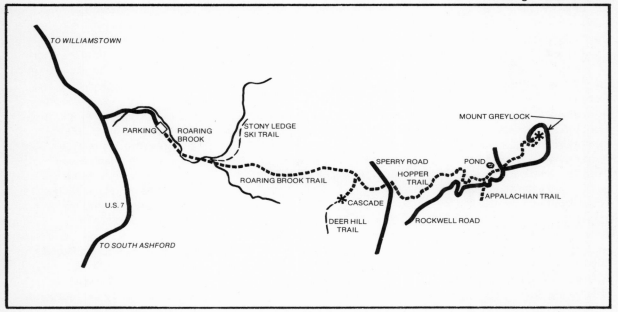

This mountain bears the name of a proud and fierce Indian chief called Grey-Lock by the English because of his gray lock of hair. His tribe's hunting grounds originally included land in the vicinity of Northfield and Springfield. In 1675, advancing white men attacked Grey-Lock's Agawam warriors and forced them northward. The chief reestablished his people on the lower Missiquoi River in Champlain Valley where they built Fort St. Regis. Justly vengeful, Grey-Lock returned three times to his native Agawam hunting grounds to ravage the English settlements at Northfield. His tribesmen guarded their new hunting grounds at Mount Greylock and roamed the trails at its base, which probably accounted for the legend that any Christian who attempted to ascend the mountain would never return.

Today, tourists and hikers can climb this highest peak in Massachusetts with considerably less trepidation. A 100-foot war memorial rises above Mount Greylock's 3,491-foot summit. From the observation platform a 360-degree view unfolds across five states.

This combination of trails leading from the west to Mount Greylock's summit includes a stop at the Heart of Greylock, a cascading waterfall tucked within the mountain's wilderness. Much of the climb follows a relentless, uphill grade.

On US 7, drive either 1.4 miles south from the junction of route 7 and Mass 43 in South Williamstown or .6 miles north from the South Ashford–Williamstown line. Turn east onto the narrow gravel road at the Roaring Brook Trail sign. Follow it ½ mile to the parking area next to the water on the left.

Walk up the road to the fork where white blazes guide you left (beside Roaring Brook). The rough dirt road crosses the brook and narrows to pass between heavy growths of day lily, common buttercup, and purple flowering raspberry.

Roaring Brook drops below as the trail climbs up to the left. Leveling out under low-hanging hemlocks, the way crosses the brook a second time. Take either fork ahead; they rejoin quickly.

After crossing the brook one more time, bear right at the next fork and step over a smaller tributary. Swing left at the Roaring Brook Trail sign and begin a long, steep climb over the wide, rocky trail. Hardwoods and spruces fill the forest. You'll want to pace yourself during this initial, rugged ascent. If you think like a "three-miler" rather than a sprinter (and also take heart-slowing stops), this jaunt will be more enjoyable.

As you climb higher the grade lessens somewhat. Evergreens spill their needles to cushion the path. The trail narrows to knife its way through thick side growth of ferns and blackberries. Creeping grasses swish over boot tops.

After 1.4 miles of hiking, you reach the junction with the Deer Hill Trail. For the moment, leave the Roaring Brook Trail and follow this orange-blazed, soft path down a precipitous hillside to the right for a ¼-mile side trip to the Heart of Greylock. The route leads you first to a bridge over a brook where you'll have a preview of the beautiful waterfall below. (The Circular Trail exits left.)

Bear right at the bridge, following the Deer Hill Trail down the extremely steep slope. Your ears (and the curving path) will guide you to the Heart of Greylock. A fifty-foot cascade suddenly looms above as the path swings close to parallel the brook. Gushing streams of water slide, bounce, and splash over mossy rocks. Individual streamlets form fluid icicles which disappear into the frothy basin below.

Return to the Roaring Brook Trail and walk right across the footbridge. Winding its way up to Sperry Campground, the trail turns left to cross another bridge over a brook. Bear right at the fork.

Turn right onto Sperry Road and walk 100 yards to the sign for the Hopper Trail. Follow the path (left) uphill into the woods. Blue dots above orange guide the way.

The Hopper Trail climbs a moderate grade past wood asters, wood sorrel, and clubmoss. Bearing left at a fork,

Mount Greylock

the path climbs steeply over roots and ledge. Farther on, it bears left as another trail forks to the right (watch here on your return trip for the overhead sign pointing right to the Hopper Trail).

After 2.6 miles, swing sharply right on the Hopper Trail (the Overlook Trail leads left here) and climb easily to Rockwell Road. Turn left just before the blacktop road and quickly left again at a summit sign. The narrow, grassy path leads to Rockwell Road after 2.8 miles of hiking.

Walk uphill to the left 200 feet (opposite the Cheshire Harbor Trail) and turn left onto the white-blazed Appalachian Trail. This narrow, damp route climbs uphill, bends right, and suddenly arrives at the edge of a picturesque little pond. A small wooden hut atop a stone foundation casts its reflection across the quiet, tree-ringed waters.

Skirting the pond's eastern edge, the Appalachian Trail meets the Rockwell Road–Notch Road junction. Just beyond the intersection, turn off

Rockwell Road onto the white-blazed path climbing up to the left. This steep, rocky route passes a TV tower and intersects the summit road. Turn right on the road to Bascomb Lodge and the observation tower beyond.

Both tower and lodge are open daily, 10 a.m. to dark, from May 15 to October 15 (you may eat, rest, buy souvenirs, and stay overnight at the lodge). The present tower was erected

in 1933 by the state as a memorial to its war dead. It was condemned in 1960 and dismantled and rebuilt (in 1974) at a cost of $430,000.

Return 2.8 miles by the same route (excluding the Deer Hill Trail spur) to your car.

Mount Greylock

Honwee Mountain

43.   Honwee Mountain

Class: III
Elevation: 2,313 feet
Vertical rise: 1,063 feet
Distance (around loop): 2.8 miles
Hiking time: 1½ hours

Before white men settled in the Berkshire Hills, the Indians had given descriptive names to topographical features. When the early settlers began moving west in the middle 1700s, they accepted some of the existing mountain names, but more often changed them to reflect local associations. Honwee ("the tall one") retains its original—and highly appropriate—Indian name.

From its junction with Mass 9 at the Pittsfield Common, drive west for 2.6 miles on West Street. Turn right onto Churchill Street and follow it 1.6 miles (passing Cascade Road) to Cascade Street. Turn left here, following signs to the Pittsfield State Forest. Continue straight from the park entrance past the Region 5 headquarters building to the Forest Fire headquarters. A parking area is diagonally across the road near a small pond.

The Honwee Circuit Trail begins on the other side of the road, 100 feet to the left of the small wooden warming hut.

Red-spotted newt

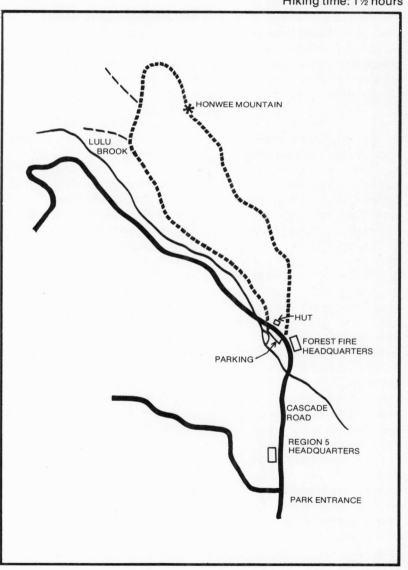

Honwee Mountain

The gravel road leads up through hardwood forests carpeted with ferns and ground pine. Passing an old overgrown road on the right, it climbs gradually uphill.

The sound of rushing water drifts upward from the valley. Soon you can look down to Lulu Brook and its whirling, slithering movements. The soothing sound of flowing water will accompany you much of the way to Honwee Mountain's summit.

This portion of the Honwee Circuit Trail is long, straight, and moderate to steep.

The road gets a bit rockier just before it reaches another side trail opposite a huge birch tree at 1.1 mile. Turn right onto this narrow path and climb to the trail fork 500 feet ahead. Bear right here, following the sign identifying the Honwee Circuit Trail. The path narrows and climbs steeply before leveling out. Passing along the flat ridgeline, it crosses the tree-enclosed summit of Honwee Mountain.

Hordes of wild berry bushes await your arrival at the summit. Their arching branches reach across the trail, threatening to slow your progress.

During much of the relaxing descent you'll see sharp-leaved wood asters. If you're descending just after a spring or summer rain, you'll see bright orange salamanders lying conspicuously against the trail's drabber greens and browns. These are red-spotted newts, remarkable little creatures which, when born, breathe in water like fish. They quickly lose gills and fins, however, and begin their "land" lives. Gay colors appear; the rough skin turns orange, and vermillion spots outlined in black line the spine on each side. The newt lives on land, sometimes far from the nearest water, for two and one half years, usually remaining hidden among leaves or moss,

or in decaying wood. Only after a rain is it able to go forth without drying up and dying. At the end of its sub-adult stage, the newt instinctively returns to water, where it reconverts to a gill breather and changes to a more protective olive green color.

The path descends more steeply and widens to become an old road. Resuming its gradual ways, it becomes grassier before returning you to the road beside the Forest Fire headquarters. Your car is across the street.

Honwee Mountain

44.   Smith Mountain

Class: II
Elevation: 2,170 feet
Vertical rise: 530 feet
Distance (round trip): 1.9 miles
Hiking time: 1 hour

This out-of-the-way hike up Smith Mountain in Hancock is not as prosaic as the name suggests. Winding wooded roads wander pleasantly to the summit, which is covered by trees and shrubs. A bare, elevated knoll on the return trail gives opportunities for views of neighboring peaks. Bring something that can be readily converted into a container, like a canteen or hat: in season, berries thrive along the way.

To start the hike, drive west on West Street from its junction with Mass 9 at the Pittsfield Common. This paved street eventually becomes Lebanon Springs Road and changes to a rough dirt road. Drive a total of 5.4 miles to where the Taconic Skyline Trail (an old wooded road at this point) crosses Lebanon Springs Road. Park on the side of the road here.

Turn north onto the Taconic Skyline Trail. The moderate but steady climb begins right away as you follow occasional circular white blazes. Gray birches grow along the old road. (In abandoned pastures, these trees herald the advent of white pine. They disappear

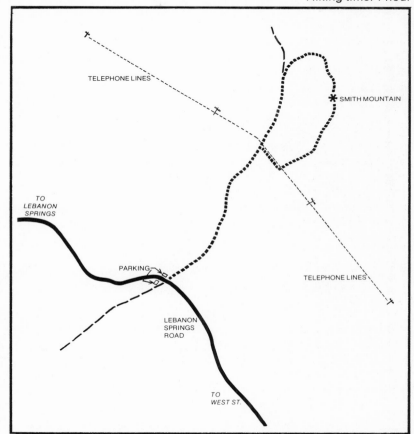

as the pine matures.)

As the trail continues its steady climb, listen and watch for the red-eyed vireo. This bird's song, an endless series of only slightly varied phrases, has earned it the nickname "preacher." A black-bordered, white stripe over the eye, blue gray cap, and greenish body (the red eyes are of little value as fieldmarks) make it easy to identify.

At ½ mile, you pass beneath telephone lines and continue straight for .2 miles to a fork. Follow the right path and ascend on a grassier old lane.

For the next ½ mile be alert for berries in the thick growth to the sides of the trail. Near Smith Mountain's summit, hay-scented fern competes with assorted berry bushes for growing room.

After 1 mile of hiking you reach the summit. The path levels as low shrubs and bushes allow unlimited views upward, but not outward. As you continue, gradually descending southwestward on the grassy road, look ahead to the rolling hilltops and mountains coming into sight. You reach telephone lines .3 miles below the summit, at an open, ledged area. You'll have your best views (especially to the south) of the hike from this vantage point.

Turn right and follow the path beneath the telephone lines back to the Taconic Skyline Trail. Queen Anne's lace blooms profusely beside the path. (The plant is pleasant in this setting, but dairy farmers struggle to keep it out of their fields. When cows feed on it, their milk takes on an unpleasant taste.)

Turn left at the Taconic Skyline Trail for the ½-mile return route to your car.

Fireweed

Smith Mountain

Pleasant Valley Sanctuary

45. Pleasant Valley Sanctuary

Class: I
Distance (round trip): 1½ miles
Hiking time: ¾ hour

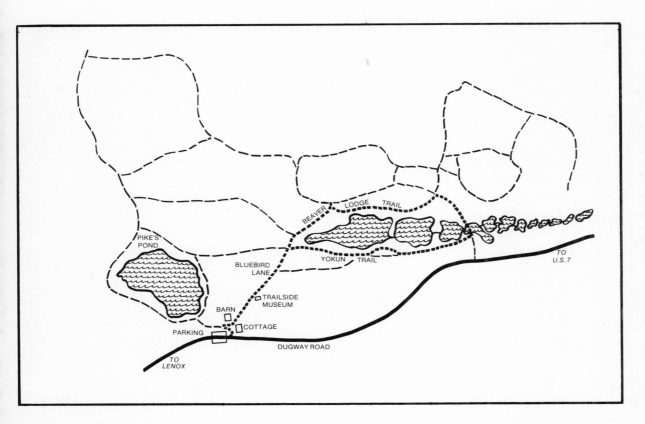

Beavers were first introduced to the Pleasant Valley Sanctuary in 1932. Since then they have moved about regularly but remained within the sanctuary. Although there is no predicting which pond they will

Animal tracks

inhabit in any given year, sanctuary personnel always know their whereabouts and guarantee sightings after 7 p.m. (Early-morning visitors might also see these furry rodents swimming and tail-slapping about.)

You'll see lodges, dams, and cuttings as you walk near the

ponds within the Beaver Pond Circuit route. Muskrats and mink live, and can occasionally be seen, at the beaver ponds along Yokun Brook. Beavers initially move into a suitable area and begin constructing a dam and lodge. Muskrats are attracted to the newly created habitat and sometimes take up residence on top of beaver lodges. Mink complete the sequence by arriving to prey upon the muskrats—one of their favorite foods.

This Beaver Pond Circuit walk introduces you to only a portion of the sanctuary's more than twelve miles of trails (from leisurely walks to challenging climbs) over typical Berkshire meadows, upland pastures, and mountains.

To reach the parking area, drive 1.8 miles south on US 7 from the Pittsfield-Lenox line. Turn west at the Pleasant Valley Sanctuary sign (opposite the Holiday Inn) onto Dugway Road. Follow this route 1.6 miles to the parking area at the sanctuary entrance. Parking rates for those who are not members of the Massachusetts Audubon Society are 50¢ per two-wheel vehicle, 50¢ per pedestrian, $1 per four-wheel vehicle, and $10 per bus.

In addition to beavers, more than sixty species of birds nest within the sanctuary's one-square-mile territory. Double that number use the area as a stopping place during migra-

tions. Houses and feeding stations attract many of the birds close enough to be observed from the trails.

After registering, go straight ahead (between the cottage and barn) to the Trailside Museum. A stop at this exciting facility is a must, now or on the return trip. Live and stuffed animals, three-dimensional displays, electronic nature games, and graphically-illustrated wall boards make this a stimulating educational experience.

Continue straight ahead on Bluebird Lane (keeping the museum on the right) past fields lined with bird houses and red pine boughs. Bear left at the fork ahead, staying on Bluebird Lane. Follow it downhill and tunnel into the maples along the bottom of the incline.

Blue blazes, a rooty path, and brown pine needles bring you to a trail intersection. Go right onto Yokun Trail. The stillness of this shady dirt path should awaken your senses to the movements of nearby residents. Turn left onto the

spur trail which takes you closer to the beaver ponds.

Short-tailed shrews are among the many smaller inhabitants of this area. They are predominantly-nocturnal animals who, like field mice, use runways through moss and other vegetation.

Other short spurs take you closer to the water's edge before the Yokun Trail stops at a T intersection. Go left across the old log footbridge. Look down at the semi-camouflaged frogs sitting half out of the water. With each sweep of the pond your eyes will locate more of these bubble-eyed amphibians.

Moving back into thick woods, turn left at the trail junction ahead onto the Beaver Lodge Trail. This path winds through forests, draws near the water, and finally enters stately hemlock-dominated woods before crossing two streams and returning you to the junction of Yokun Trail and Bluebird Lane.

Retrace your uphill route on Bluebird Lane back to the parking area.

Pleasant Valley Sanctuary

46. Lenox Mountain

Class: III
Elevation: 2,123 feet
Vertical rise: 813 feet
Distance (round trip): 2.8 miles
Hiking time: 1¾ hours

Lenox Mountain was named for the town of Lenox, which in turn had taken its name from Charles Lenox, Duke of Richmond, who championed our colonial rights. The town is best-known as the site of Tanglewood, summer home of the Boston Symphony Orchestra; the mountain is memorable for the 360-degree view from the tower on its summit.

The Lenox Mountain fire tower is the "key tower" for its district. Each key tower is manned continuously. Other towers in each district are not staffed unless there is serious forest-fire danger. Fire-surveillance planes are taking over the duties formerly held by tower spotters.

Reach the start of this hike by following the directions to Pleasant Valley Sanctuary (Hike 45). Your route to the summit takes you for a more rigorous outing than the sanctuary's other trails. Parts of the first half of this climb are quite steep and demanding.

From the parking lot walk straight ahead (pay the sanctuary fee), between the cottage

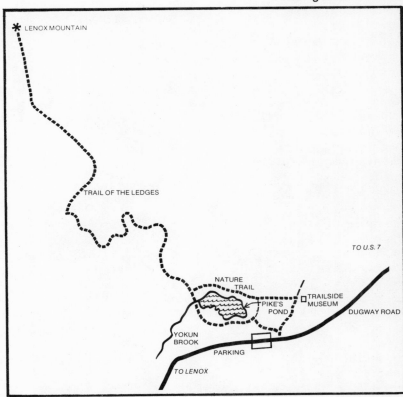

and barn, to the Trailside Museum. Here a relief map puts the area into topographical perspective. Turn left (west) in front of the museum and walk across the field toward the start of the Nature Trail.

Stay right at the next fork and follow the northern shore of

Pike's Pond. You'll see the seemingly random mass of sticks placed by beavers to heighten the water level. Turn right onto the blue-blazed Trail of the Ledges (indicated by the "To Firetower" sign). Blue blazes mark your trip up the mountain; yellow blazes will guide you back down the

Lenox Mountain

Lenox Mountain

same trail. Disregard the older, red blazes when they disagree with the direction shown by the blue or yellow blazes.

Watch for Indian pipe with its waxy white scales arranged in spiral fashion around the fleshy stem.

At .4 miles the Ravine Trail branches right. Continue straight, climbing steeply over ledge covered by moss and lichen. Serpentine roots serve as stairs up some of the steeper sections. Pockets in the slippery ledge offer foot and finger holds when needed. Mountain laurel decorates the trailsides with color and fragrance in May and June.

After .7 miles of walking you reach the Fairviews, a southeast overlook to nearby wooded hilltops. Here the Laurel Trail leads straight ahead. Turn sharply left, following the blue-blazed Lenox Mountain fire tower trail.

Mountain laurel and hobblebush cause the path to narrow. Blue-

bead lily raises its foot-high stalk of berries amidst wide, glossy leaves. Lemon-yellow, miniature lilies precede the brilliantly-hued fruit.

Most of the steep climbing lies behind you as you pass through the hushed light of a hemlock grove. After a sharp swing to the left (marked by double blue blazes), you walk out into an open area for views of the countryside to the east and northeast.

Alternately climbing and descending for short stretches, the way passes by smooth beech trees scarred by name carvers.

Soon after visiting a third ledged overlook (this one faces east), you emerge from the woods onto a wide, grassy, road. In front of you a chain-link fence encloses cable television trans-

mission towers. Swing right and walk to the Lenox Mountain fire tower. Climb to the top for a full circle of views; on clear days the horizon extends to forty miles.

Return by the same trail, watching carefully for the yellow blazes. At the junction with the Nature Trail, bear right around Pike's Pond. This half of the Nature Trail loop ends at the parking lot.

Indian Pipe

Lenox Mountain

Squaw Peak

47.   Squaw Peak

Class: III
Elevation: 1,642 feet
Vertical rise: 762 feet
Distance (round trip): 2.3 miles
Hiking time: 1½ hours

Monument Mountain and its summit, Squaw Peak, derived their names from Indian legend. Oucannawa, a beautiful girl from the Stockbridge tribe, fell in love with her cousin, Chief Salouch. Tribal law forbade the marriage. So Oucannawa jumped to her death from the highest cliff. Her burial place at the bottom of the precipice is marked by a cairn, created over the years by Indians who deposited a stone at the spot each time they passed.

On US 7, drive 4 miles north from Great Barrington or 2.5 miles south from Stockbridge to the parking and picnic area at the sign for Monument Mountain Reservation.

The Hickey Trail starts to the right of the trail sign at the front of the picnic area. Go north (right) behind the cement-block latrine. White blazes mark the wide, flat path. Climbing more steeply through pines, you bear right at a fork and pass by an old stone well on the left. Go left at the next T intersection, then swing right at a fork.

View of Squaw Peak

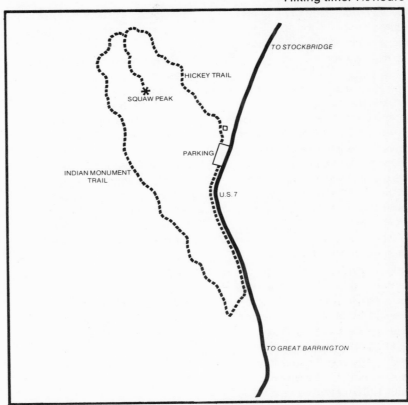

Listen for the eastern wood pewee's slurred song: *pee-ah-wee, pee-ah.* (Just after daybreak and at twilight it includes a third call: *bi-de-dee.*) Lack of eye rings and prominent white wing bars distinguish this dark brown bird from the eastern phoebe. The pewee perches well up in trees waiting to ambush insects.

Step over rows of stones placed across the trail to divert run-off. Laurel and hemlock squeeze the sides of the narrowing path. Go right at the next intersection.

Soon after passing a looming glacial boulder on the left,

the way swings left to parallel a stream-carved gorge. Hemlocks crown the slanting banks above the water.

You make a switch back to the left and then turn left at a T intersection, now hiking southerly toward the summit. A marker (erected by the park's donor, Helen C. Butler, in memory of her sister Rosalie) is to the right of the trail. The path fills with sand and small stones as you climb higher.

After mounting shelves of ledge, you reach a cliff-top vantage point with views across mountain tops in a wide, easterly sweep. From this rock balcony you can see Mount Wilcox (2,112 feet) to the southeast and 1,820-foot Hunger Mountain beyond. Beartown Mountain (1,870 feet) rises in the near east; farther east you can see the top of 1,930-foot Kingsbury Mountain. Look northeast to 2,178-foot Becket Mountain and north to Lenox Mountain (2,123 feet).

Push your way through stands of pitch pine. Thick, rough, deeply-wrinkled bark covers this scrubby tree. Abundant on Cape Cod, it is less common in the western part of the state.

Continue along the ridgeline to Squaw Peak for full-circle views of the surrounding country-side. From the summit you can look northwest to 1,933-foot Tom Ball Mountain.

Retrace your steps from the summit (passing the memorial stone on the left) to the point where white-blazed trails fork. The right fork is your original route, the Hickey Trail. Go left onto the (unsigned) Indian Monument Trail.

This wide, gradually descending route passes through young woods. Keep an eye out for the unusual, all-white Indian pipe. Leaf-covered, moist, trailside soil provides ideal habitat for this parasitic plant.

Reaching a fork, the trail bears left, guided by white blazes. You hear the traffic on route 7 just before making a looping switchback to the left and following the trail down to the highway. Turn left and walk the ¼ mile along route 7 to your car.

Squaw Peak

48.   **Mount Wilcox**

Class: II
Elevation: 2,112 feet
Vertical rise: 552 feet
Distance (round trip): 4.4 miles
Hiking time: 2¼ hours

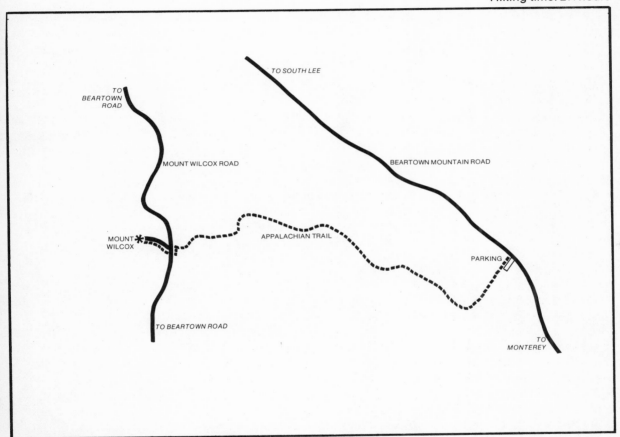

The ascent to Mount Wilcox via the Appalachian Trail from the east provides one of the easiest climbs to a summit in the entire state. The route rises gently in places, but passes mostly over long, level stretches of trail; in more than 2 miles, this portion of the Appalachian Trail rises only 462 feet.

This hike combines relaxing terrain with other lures: wild flowers in the spring; cool shaded paths in the hot summer months; colorful hardwood forests in the fall; and an easy snowshoe trek in the winter. Trees have closed off the summit views and the fire tower is no longer

Mount Wilcox

open to the public. Enjoyment comes, not at the top, but along the way.

From the center of Monterey, drive north on the Tyringham Road .6 miles to a fork. Bear left on Beartown Mountain Road and follow its eventually-graveled surface 2.4 miles to the Appalachian Trail (white blazes) which leads left (west) down an old road. Park along the widened sides of this grassy woods road.

The trail leads easily up a slight grade under the arching branches of shade trees. Winding through hardwood forests, the way suddenly reaches a dense stand of spiny spruces. Sunlight scarcely penetrates the concentrated grouping of bare boughs and skeletal trunks. Needles from the green uppermost sections make a comfortable carpet on the path beneath.

Roots fill the road as it swings right and climbs gently through corridors of eerie evergreens closing in from both sides. A monochromatic, reddish-gray tinge permeates the forest.

Trees, roots, and trail blend duskily together.

The primitive spiny spruces fade away as the trail approaches a stone wall on the left. Entering a less somber, spruce-lined arbor, you climb gradually as your shoes scuff through thick evergreen spills.

Hardwoods resume their dominance and give the trail more breathing room. The path continues its unusually level route, then dips to cross a brook after 1¼ miles of hiking.

You'll see common flickers flit from tree to tree. Watch for the bird's white rump and gold wing linings in flight. A black throat patch, red streak on the nape of the neck, and speckled breast help identify this handsome woodpecker. Its call is a loud, repeated *wicker.*

The trail narrows and becomes rockier before leveling out to pass ferns, shrubs, and lilies. Downed tree trunks along the way support colonies of multi-zoned polystictus fungus. Thin, leathery, fan-shaped brackets cluster on the dead wood. Concentric bands of varied somber colors account for this polypore's nickname, "turkey tails."

After 2 miles of walking, you step up onto Mount Wilcox Road. Walk left 100 feet and make a sharp switchback right onto the dirt road leading to the summit. A breezy, open area near the fire tower invites you to stop and rest before returning to your car by the same route you ascended.

Gnarled Birches

Mount Wilcox

49.   Bash Bish Falls

Class: IV
Elevation: 1,270 feet
Vertical rise: 520 feet
Distance (to falls and back): .8 miles
Hiking time: ¾ hour

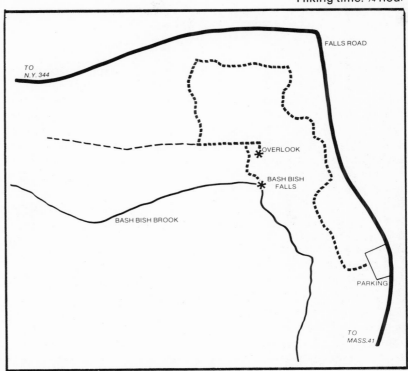

The state's most spectacular waterfalls are located in the tiny town of Mount Washington. Nestled snugly near the New York and Connecticut state lines, Mount Washington's approximately fifty residents are better known for their voting practices than for the majestic falls within the town's boundaries. The town's voters try to be—and usually are—the first in the United States to report presidential election returns.

According to Indian legend, the spirit profile of White Swan, a beautiful maiden, can be seen in the pool below Bash Bish Falls. Because she was childless, her husband took another wife. Heartbroken, White Swan took to gazing into the waters below the falls for long periods of time. One day the voice of her mother, a witch who lived beneath the falls, called to her. White Swan jumped from the cliff and plunged into the water just as her husband arrived on the scene. He too jumped in a vain effort to save the woman. The brave's body was

Bash Bish Falls

later found, but not White Swan's. The legend has it that she and her mother live behind the falls and that on moonlit nights White Swan can be seen smiling in the clear pool.

Bash Bish may be an onomatopoeic Indian name, suggested by the sound of falling waters. But in his *History of the Township of Mount Washington, Mass.,* compiled in 1950, Weldon B. Hestor suggests that the name is of vulgar origin. Mr. Hestor doesn't inform his readers which Anglo-Saxon colloquialism he has in mind, so your guess is as good as ours.

Rain and melting snow swell

Bash Bish Brook in the spring, causing a thundering cascade over the falls. That is the ideal time to view the spectacle. But even in dry seasons, sufficient water pours through the high-walled canyon to make a visit worthwhile.

From the junction of Mass 23 and Mass 41 in South Egremont, drive south a short distance on route 41 to the fork. Go right, following signs to Mount Everett and Mount Washington. Along this route you will see signs for Bash Bish Falls. Follow them to the parking area.

Blue and white triangular trail signs direct you to the right from the rear of the parking lot. Skirting boulders, the path drops quickly through birches and hemlocks. Much of this route to the falls is quite steep; move carefully, especially when crossing loose rocks.

The trail winds down, levels somewhat, and becomes rocky as it swings sharply left to cross a brook clogged with logs and stones. The well-marked path slices across a sloping hillside before curling gradually downward through young, feathery hemlocks.

You begin to hear the distant, muffled roar of the falls far below. The rocky path leads steadily downward. Water sounds grow louder. You turn sharply left. Expectations heighten with the increasing roar, but thick trees still conceal your objective.

After stepping down to an old road, you turn left and suddenly arrive at the falls. (Watch your step if you descend to the base of the falls from this overlook.) Imposing, tree-rimmed canyon walls rise above the falls.

Unseen water courses through an elevated gorge to reach the rocks atop the falls. It swirls down, around, and through jumbled boulders before cascading into White Swan's quiet pool below. Smooth stone attests to the water's pounding force.

Return by the same route to your car.

Bash Bish Falls

50. Mount Everett

Class: III
Elevation: 2,602 feet
Vertical rise: 1,682 feet
Distance (round trip): 5.8 miles
Hiking time: 3 hours

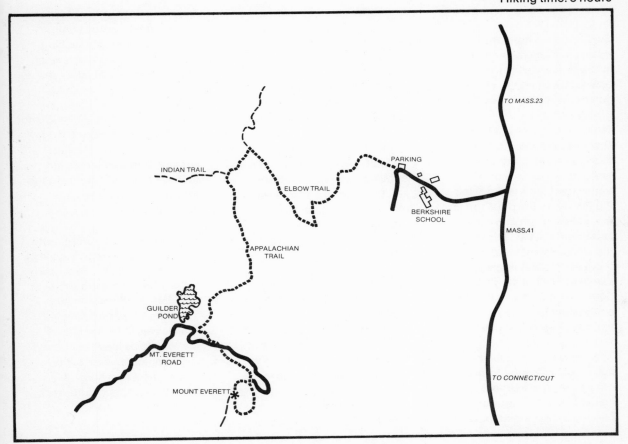

Old upland farms, stone walls, spruce stands, primeval hemlock, huckleberries, blueberries, and Guilder Pond—the highest natural body of water in the state—are just some of the attractions which crowd Mount Everett's slopes.

Walter Prichard Eaton was an early protector of the mountain's ecology. In November 1927, when fall floods made the summit road's final 2/3 mile impassable, he fought to close the motor road to the summit. He suggested that money allocated to repair the road be used to establish a long hiking trail over Mount Everett which could become a link in the Appala-

Mount Everett

chian Trail.

Eaton won his fight; the road was never repaired and the trail which is part of this hike now forms an important section of the Appalachian Trail.

From the junction of Mass 41 and Mass 23 in South Egremont, go south on route 41 for 3.2 miles to the signed entrance road (on the right) for the Berkshire School. Turn in, drive past the athletic fields, and turn right. Continue toward the long, cement building. Drive between this building and the painted brick building on its right. Go uphill past a house on the right to a sharp bend in the road. Park in the clearing.

The well-trodden, unblazed Elbow Trail leads west from the corner. Beyond a brook, you maintain a steady upward grade, passing between hemlocks and then beneath a hardwood canopy on a wider path. Narrowing again, the way slabs diagonally up the slope.

Pert, sociable black-capped chickadees may congregate in overhead branches to noisily inspect you.

At .6 miles the trail makes a switchback to the right. Edging beside mounds of ledge, it levels out a bit and descends gradually along a hemlock-lined lane. Mountain laurel hugs the path as you make your way over a rockier trail.

After 1.1 miles of hiking you turn left onto the white-blazed Appalachian Trail. (Note this junction well so that you will recognize it on your return trip.) Cross a brook and follow the blazes sharply right, climbing more steeply.

You reach the picnic area just above Guilder Pond after 2¼ miles of hiking. After winding back into thick woods, climb the embankment onto the gravel summit road. Go left, following the road for 100 feet, then turn right into the woods again. The trail parallels the road, swings right beneath power lines, and climbs up over a jumble of large boulders to a graveled clearing (part of the abandoned summit road). Walk ahead on the old road to a hairpin turn. Follow the white blazes straight here.

Berry bushes and scrub oak

threaten to choke this slender trail before it emerges onto open ledge with far-reaching views below. Look a little west of south to the distinctive shape of Connecticut's Twin Lakes, Washining (with an evergreen peninsula) and Washinee. Climb up over quartz-streaked ledge to Mount Everett's spacious summit. The tower is closed to the public, but a walk around the area will produce a full circle of views.

You can vary your return route for a short distance by walking northeast from the tower down the remains of the old summit road. Wind down to where the white-blazed Appalachian Trail leaves the left side of the road to descend over the large boulders beneath the power line. From here, retrace your original route back to your car.

View from Mount Everett

Mount Everett